ORCHID GROWING BASICS

ORCHID GROWING BASICS

Dr. Gustav Schoser

Sterling Publishing Co., Inc. New York

Photo credits
Title Photo: Hermann Eisenbeis, Egling, Germany.
Photos:
Johannes Apel, Baden-Baden: pgs. 3, 62, 76, 102, 105, 113.
Helmut Bechtel, Heimbach: pgs. 8, 13, 14, 17, 19, 22, 53, 68 top, 82, 84, 89, 91 below, 94, 96, 98 below, 100, 103 top, 104, 106, 109, 111 top, 117 top, 121 below, 122.
Rolf Blaich, Ilbesheim: pgs. 18, 65 below, 77, 97.
Ernst Bormann, Duisburg (Photo: Jürgen Kipf, Wiesbaden): pgs. 30, 31.
Klaus Finn, Hannover: pg. 6.
Archiv Falken-Verlag GmbH, Niedernhausen/Rolf Blaich, Ilbesheim: pgs. 10, 24, 29, 56, 63 below, 64, 66 below, 70, 71, 74, 86, 88, 91 top, 101, 107, 108, 111 below, 118 right.
Fleurop GmbH, Dirc Nienhaus, Berlin: pg. 115.
Kuno Krieger, Herdecke/Ruhr: pgs. 14 right, 16, 25, 43, 44, 46, 50 top, 51, 54, 55, 58, 60, 61, 63, 65 top, 78, 80, 81, 103 below, 117 below, 119, 120, 121 top, 123.
Eberhard Morell, Dreieich: pgs. 50 below, 57 below.
Rudolf Schmied, Friedberg: pgs. 69, 85.
Dr. Gustav Schoser, Frankfurt: pgs. 12, 48, 49, 57 top, 59, 66 top, 67, 73, 75, 87, 92, 93, 99, 110, 118 left.
Drawings: Regina Brendel, Aarbergen-Panrod.

Library of Congress Cataloging-in-Publication Data

Schoser, Gustav.
   [Orchideen. English]
   Orchid growing basics / Gustav Schoser.
      p.   cm.
   Includes index.
   ISBN 0-8069-0362-7
   1. Orchid culture. I. Title.
SB409.S3713   1993
635.9'3415—dc20   93-24785
                                       CIP

20 19 18 17 16 15 14 16 12 11

Published in 1993 by Sterling Publishing Company, Inc.
387 Park Avenue South, New York, N.Y. 10016
Originally published and © 1991 in Germany by
Falken-Verlag GmbH, 6272 Niedernhausen/Ts.,
under the title *Orchideen: Lebensraum, Kultur, Anzucht und Pflege*
English translation © 1993 by Sterling Publishing Company, Inc.
Distributed in Canada by Sterling Publishing
% Canadian Manda Group, P.O. Box 920, Station U
Toronto, Ontario, Canada M8Z 5P9
Distributed in Great Britain and Europe by Cassell PLC
Villiers House, 41/47 Strand, London WC2N 5JE, England
Distributed in Australia by Capricorn Link (Australia) Pty Ltd.
P.O. Box 704, Windsor, NSW 2756 Australia
Printed in Hong Kong
All rights reserved

Sterling ISBN 0-8069-0362-7

Contents

Preface

Dear Orchid lover,

The popularity of orchids is one of the reasons why they are in trouble in their natural habitat. Many species are threatened with extinction. In the 1970s, many countries signed a species protection law in Washington. The law controls the selling of this endangered plant. Most of the orchids introduced in this book are governed by that agreement. When you buy orchids commercially, make sure that they come from a company that is a reputable, recognized breeder and that the orchids have been grown from seeds or by division. You will not only have obeyed the law, you will also have contributed to the preservation of a precious, valuable, and increasingly rare plant. To avoid any conflict, you can simply enjoy the many wonderful hybrids available.

Thank you for your understanding!
Yours,

Gustav Schoser

Gustav Schoser

In the case of hybrids, such as this Paphiopedilum rosetti, there is no danger that any laws have been violated.

The Peculiar World of Orchids

It isn't surprising that the orchid, with all its many varieties, continues to fascinate people all over the world. Orchids are captivating, exotic, and gloriously colorful plants. However, the orchid family consists of more than exotic beauties; it includes many other small, unassuming plants that grow in fields, in meadows, and in woodlands.

The testicle-shaped root of these flowers gives orchids their name.

What Is an Orchid?

The word orchid comes from the Greek *orchis*, meaning testicles, because the roots of a wild orchid resemble testicles.

All orchids belong to the family of Orchidaceae, one of the largest of all the plant families. Some experts believe that there are at least 25,000 wild species that belong to 750 different genera, some of which genera consist of only one species.

The number of hybrids, the result of crossbreeding, is at least that large. Hybrids are a good example of the diversity and richness in shape and structure of the orchid.

Orchids are plants that have a single germ cell. They are particularly varied in the shape of their blossoms. Some have an unusual capacity to adapt to a given environment and to specific conditions.

A predisposition to hybridization (crossbreeding) is an indication that a young plant species is at the height of its development.

What's in a Name?

Linnaeus established the modern scientific system of binomial nomenclature for plant names. This method consists of the name of the genus, followed by the name of the species, and then the name of the person who first described the plant; for example: *Paphiopedilum* (genus) *sukhakulii* (species) Schoser and Senghas (describers of the plant in 1965). Added to this basic format are subspecies, varieties, and structures. Varieties that are the result of cultivation are called **types**.

When plants are the result of hybridization of two or more genera, their names are combined, or a new name is formed by adding the suffix "ara" (see box at right). There are approximately 300 genera hybrids in the orchid family.

All offspring of a hybridized plant are called **Grex**. They often show a rather large variety of appearances. If one particular plant is chosen from these for propagation, we have a clone, which can only be reproduced through vegetative multiplication. Such a clone, for instance, is *Vuylstekeara Cambria "Plush"* (1. name: genera hybrid; 2. Grex name; 3. clone name).

In addition to genera hybrids, we also have hybridization of different species of a genus, the so-called primary hybrids.

The names of Grex and clones are capitalized; the names of species and species hybrids are not.

Examples of naming genera hybrids:
1. *Brassavola* × *Cattleya* × *Laelia* = *Brassolaeliocattleya (Blc)*
2. *Brassavola* × *Cattleya* × *Laelia* × *Sophronitis* = *Potinara*
3. *Cochlioda* × *Miltonia* × *Odontoglossum* = *Vuylstekeara*

Structure of the Orchid Plant

The orchid plant consists of roots, shoots, and leaves. It is possible to distinguish between two different growth patterns. The first type is **monopodial** (single stem). In this type, the orchid grows in one direction—upright. New leaves grow

Brassolaeliocattleya, a hybridization of three genera

from the tip of the axis. Rows of leaves are arranged, always two opposite each other, along the length of the stem. Over time, the plant loses its leaves from the ground up. Either a floral axis or single flowers develop laterally at the main stem.

The roots of the monopodial orchid grow at the base of the stem. Typical of monopodial orchids are those from the *Aerangis, Phalaenopsis,* and *Vanda* genera.

The other kind of growth pattern, called **sympodial**, is much more common. It has a main axis, but it grows mostly horizontally. This type of orchid has several swollen shoots, called pseudobulbs, that are connected to each other via the main axis.

Pseudobulbs serve as reservoirs for water and nutrients for the plant. They allow the plant to survive periods of prolonged drought, an adap-

tation from the original habitat. Thus, *Paphiopedilum* doesn't have pseudobulbs, because the climate of its home is humid and does not have dry periods.

The sympodial orchid develops new shoots once a year at the base of the pseudobulb. The main stem grows at the same rate as the new shoot, developing new roots along the way.

Pseudobulbs take on different forms and sizes, from egg shapes, such as those from the genera *Lycaste* and *Odontoglossum,* and some flat shapes of the *Oncidium,* to round, such as some from the genus *Encyclia.* The pseudobulbs of the *Dendrobium* and the *Epidendrum* are rather thin and long. Single, as well as multiple, leaves develop at the tip

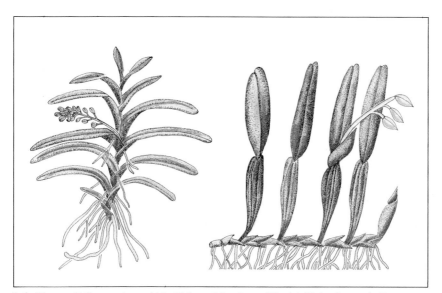

Left: Monopodially growing orchid with lateral floral axes (Vanda). Right: Sympodially growing orchid with terminal floral axes (Cattleya).

9

of the pseudobulb.

Most orchids belong to the sympodial genera, such as the *Dendrobium, Oncidium, Encyclia, Cattleya, Cymbidium,* and *Odontoglossum.*

The shape of the leaves is adapted to the different ways of life of each of the genera. Some serve as water reservoirs, and are fleshy, others are thin and large. Leaves may be reduced to the size of scales.

Parallel-veined leaves are typical of orchids. They are a sign that orchids belong to the family of monocots. (Other members of this family are the grasses and lilies.) Some leaves will remain on the stem for years; others are only present for one growing season. The color of the leaves plays an important part in adapting to the natural habitat. Colors can vary from light to dark green and to brownish red.

The relatively thick, fleshy roots serve mainly as a storage area for water and nutrients. Aerial roots have an additional layer of white

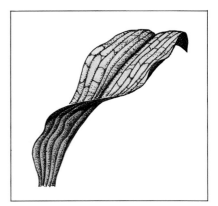

Orchid leaves have parallel veins.

cells, called velamen, that covers the outer layer of the root. The velamen is filled with air. This covering serves as a sponge for absorbing water and as protection against heat and water loss. The special protection provided by velamen is particularly important for the roots of epiphytes (see page 15) and shows the optimal adaptation of orchids to their habitat.

The variety of shapes of orchid flowers vastly outnumbers the shapes of their roots. Every conceivable type of shape and every con-

Pseudobulbs of the Maxillaria variabilis

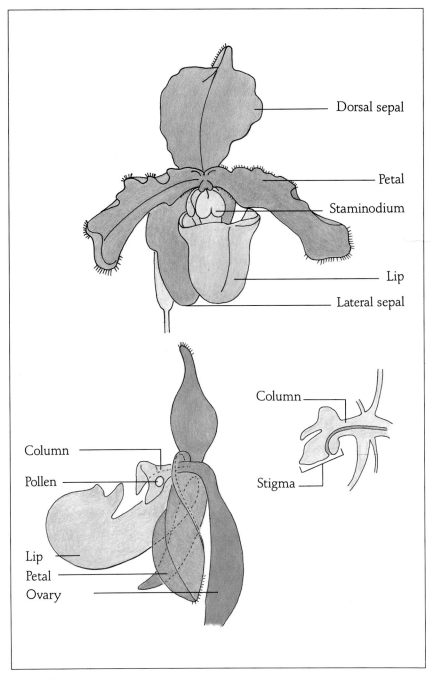

Dorsal sepal

Petal

Staminodium

Lip

Lateral sepal

Column

Pollen

Lip
Petal
Ovary

Column

Stigma

Orchid flower

ceivable color is represented. This variety helps assure that each species will continue to survive. Typically, the orchid flower (and the flower of its nearest relative, the lily) has five circles, each with three parts. The outermost circle has three leaves, called sepals, the inner circle has two leaves, called petals, and a third leaf with a very prominent shape, called the lip (labellum). These two circles of petals are followed by the stamen circle and the ovary circle.

In contrast to lilies, orchids show a distinct reduction in the stamen circle, with only one or two stamens. The fertile stamen or stamens along with the stigma and style form a special organ, called the column.

The pollen is usually caked together. During pollination, the substance is transferred as a whole.

It is possible to distinguish between two types of orchid flowers:
1. Double-stamen flowers (diandrous), with two (originally three) productive stamens.
2. Single-stamen flowers (monandrous), with one productive stamen.

Only the *Cypripedioideae*, from the genus *Paphiopedilum*, belongs to the first group. The typical characteristic is the conspicuous, slipper-

Slipper-shaped lip

12

Funnel-shaped lip

the "flag," often presents itself in most striking colors.

The lip of a monandric orchid also has a very unusual shape. Often it looks like a funnel or a tube. The lip belongs to the inner circle of the flower petals. Frequently, the colors of the lip are unusual. In the outer circle, all the sepals are shaped alike, or the dorsal sepal takes on a different shape.

Orchid flowers develop in four different styles: as single flowers, racemes (spikes), cymes (single flowers on each floral axis), or as panicles (multiple flowers on many floral axes).

Usually, all flowers open simultaneously. In some cases, however, for instance the *Phalaenopsis*, individual flowers begin to bloom one after the other, starting from the base and moving slowly upwards.

The primary reason for a flower's

like shape of the lip.

The lateral petals and the slipperlike lip are part of the inner circle. The outer circle consists of three sepals. The two lateral sepals are fused together and are usually located behind the "slipper." The upper (dorsal) sepal, sometimes called

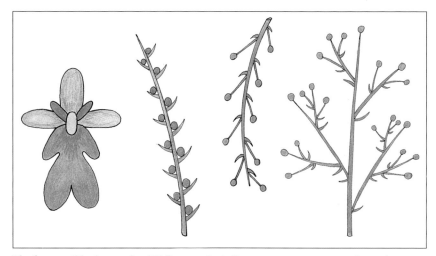

The four possible shapes of orchid flowers: single flowers; racemes, cymes, and panicles

13

existence (and for its fragrance, color, size, and life span) is to assure pollination, and, thus, the survival of the species. The flower must last long enough for insects or birds to accomplish pollination. After this has occurred, the flower wilts, and the ovary below it begins to ripen, producing the seed capsule.

The seed capsule contains the seeds. These are very light and may take a month to develop. One individual seed weighs about 1/3,500,000 of an ounce (1/1,000,000 g). It does not contain nutrition-storing tissues. The seed capsule bursts along three or six "seams," spreading an uncountable number of seeds. Because of their light weight, the seeds can be carried by the wind across great distances. The huge amount of seeds compensates for the fact that many will not find suitable ground in which to germinate.

Since orchid seeds do not have their own food-storage tissue, they form associations with fungi residing in the soil. Fungi penetrate the sprouting root system and take over the feeding of the young shoot.

This gives us some idea why it is so difficult for an orchid to germinate: it must have a chance to form an association with a fungus.

Environment and Propagation of Orchids

As is the case with all living things, the life of an orchid and the way it spreads through a region are closely related to the environment in which it lives. Orchids in moderate cli-

Neottia nidus-avis

An epiphyte

mates grow in the soil, like almost all green plants. They are called terrestrial orchids. These orchids are also found in tropical and subtropical climates. Typical representatives are the genera *Paphiopedilum, Calanthe,* and a few *Cymbidium*. Most of these orchids carry leaves, but some do not. A typical representative is *Neottia nidus-avis*.

Another "life-style" of orchids is much more common in the tropics, where many attach themselves to trees and brushes. These are called **epiphytes**. They live on other plants without doing them any harm. Epiphytic orchids left the ground because of insufficient light in unbroken tropical forests. They found optimal space in the branches of trees.

Nutrition is no problem for these plants—in a forest where rainfall occurs regularly, raindrops carry plenty of nitrogen. In addition, plant material on the branches of trees decays

much faster in tropical forests than it does in more temperate climates. This decayed matter provides sufficient food for tree-dwelling orchids.

Fleshy, rather long roots absorb nutrients and secure the plant to the tree branches. The epiphytic way of life can actually eliminate the need for leaves on an orchid. When this happens, the roots take over the role of assimilating nutrition.

Most orchids live on trees. Typical representatives of epiphytes are *Cattleya, Phalaenopsis, Oncidium,* and *Epidendrum*. Many orchids, however, live in both "worlds," as terrestrial and epiphytic orchids.

In addition, there are orchids, called lithophytes, that live on rocks. They can be found securely attached to the bark of a tree in the tropical forest and also on bare rock surfaces. Their numbers, however, are lim-

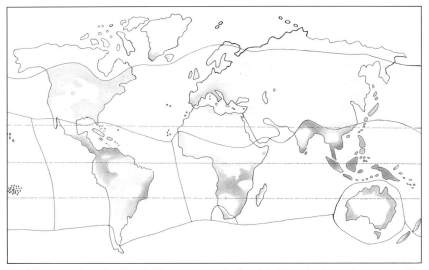

Orchids are widely distributed. They can even be found in Greenland near hot springs. The number of different species increases closer to the equator.

15

ited, probably because of the extreme conditions of such locations.

Orchids can be found all over the globe except in Antarctica, in desert regions, and at extreme elevations.

Some orchid lovers think that the orchid originated in the Asia. In fact, nowhere else on earth is there such a great variety of orchids. For instance, on that continent, the number of varieties of *Dendrobium* is said to be close to 1,400. Although the numbers decrease farther north, there are still orchids to be found in the polar regions. In the northern temperate zone, there are only about 75 different genera of orchids. The situation is similar in the southern hemisphere. In Greenland, orchids have found a home near the coast, in the vicinity of hot springs. In the southern, moderate latitudes north of Antarctica, there are 40 different genera of orchids. The numbers increase closer to the equator. Elevation also plays a role. Most orchids live at an elevation of 1,600 to 5,600 feet (500 to 1,700 m) above sea level.

The variety of locations and the adaptation of each genus to its respective environment make it very difficult to give precise instructions on care and cultivation and to use the same set of growing conditions for these very different genera.

The Tropical Regions

Since most orchids originated in tropical regions, it makes sense to begin by taking a look at the general conditions in these regions in order to understand the variety of cultivating conditions of this plant.

The tropics cover two-thirds of the entire globe. Tropical vegetation

Miltonia in a fog forest

is unsurpassed anywhere on earth in the amount of plants and the variety of their forms. Near the equator, the tropical rain forest area is called the "inner tropics." Next come the "outer tropics" and the subtropical regions.

Temperatures in the inner tropics fluctuate as widely in a day as they do in a year. The average yearly temperature is 73 to 91°F (23 to 33°C). Even during the coldest months, it does not fall below 65°F (18°C).

Rainfall is always constant, between 79 and 197 inches (2,000 and 5,000 mm) per year. Precipitation almost always occurs in the form of cloudbursts at certain times of the day. In tropical rain forests near the equator, prolonged drought does not exist.

The relative humidity changes during the course of the day with the change in temperature. The humidity is highest in the late afternoon and lowest at sunrise and immediately before the tropical rainfall, which is created by air turbulence.

Amazingly, there is always a wind present in this region, because the air masses are constantly exchanged due to temperature differences. In the tropics, the number of daylight hours is almost constant at 12. The light intensity is about the same as in temperate regions during the height of the summer, about 100,000 lux. In lowlands, however, haze and dust particles in the air reduce the light rays. In addition, the intensity of the light is diminished by the height and density of trees. Rain forests assume different forms because of the difference in the amount of precipitation and the dif-

ference in elevation. In tropical regions from 3,300 feet (1,000 m) on up, rain forests are called montane forests. It is in these forests that the greatest number of epiphytes are found. These epiphytes are present in at least as many different forms and numbers of varieties as in rain forests at lower elevations (below 3,300 feet).

Orchids in Permanently Warm, Humid Regions

The regions on both sides of the equator are those with the highest amount of precipitation. The average yearly temperature is 73 to 91°F (23 to 33°C). The difference in temperature between day and night is about 13°F (7°C). Because of the high amount of precipitation and the high temperatures, the relative humidity

Vanilla planifolia

17

is 80 to 100 percent. Orchids living in this environment have adapted well to such conditions. For instance, many species make do without pseudobulbs to serve as water reservoirs. Others have a velamen, a thick, corky tissue that holds water from cloudbursts and directs it to the roots.

Phalaenopsis and *Paphiopedilum* belong to a genus that did not develop pseudobulbs. *Phalaenopsis*, primarily an epiphyte, has aerial roots that cling tightly to the host plant. It prefers to live on the shaded, west side of a tree, where it can take advantage of the greatest amount of humidity.

The *Macodes* orchid lives primarily as a terrestrial plant, but it can also be an epiphyte. *Vanilla planifolia*, whose home is Mexico, has a root velamen and climbs high up on trees. This plant produces the vanilla pod.

Orchids in Warm Regions with Alternating Humidity

The tropical regions on either side of the equator have definite rainy and dry periods of different durations. The deficit of precipitation during the dry period is compensated for during the rest of the year. Daily temperatures average 70°F (21°C).

In most of Southeast Asia, another home of epiphytes, monsoon rains during the summer, followed by the dry, winter season, determine

Dendrobium aggregatum

18

the development of plants. The dry period (from November till January) is probably the deciding factor in when orchids bloom.

Cymbidium is an orchid typical of those found in tropical regions. This orchid is always green and has thick, fleshy bulbs and roots which are perfect for sustaining the plant through dry periods. The *Dendrobium* has a very typical pseudobulb. The small African *Ansellia* also belongs to the group of orchids living in this climate. The *Brassavola* grows both as an epiphyte and as a lithophyte at elevations up to 2,000 feet (600 m). *Brassia*, which resembles the very numerous *Odontoglossum* species, is also at home in these regions. *Phalaenopsis*, *Vanda*, and *Renanthera* usually live as epiphytes. Others, such as *Paphiopedilum*, *Spathoglottis*, *Ludisia*, and *Anectochilus*, are terrestrial plants. In the warm regions in America, where dry and humid climates alternate, there are many orchids from the *Cattleya-Laelia* group and from the *Oncidium-Ondontoglossum* group, as well as numerous other species.

Orchids Growing in Regions with Warm, Dry Days and Cool, Humid Nights

Warm and dry tropics that have cool, humid nights are different from warm regions with alternating dry and humid seasons. The difference in temperature is often as high as 25°F (12°C) during the dry period. The dry season is longer and creates an overall climate with distinct dry and rainy seasons.

Some *Cattleya* orchids have become well adapted to this climate, as

evidenced by the increase in the size of their pseudobulbs. Low nighttime temperatures of no more than 65°F (18°C) are responsible for the development of their flowers. *Laelia* also prefer this kind of climate. Some of the *Oncidium* orchids are at home here, too.

Cycnoches have long, spindle-shaped pseudobulbs and elongated leaves that die off after active growth has stopped.

Orchids in Humid, Cool Tropical Climates

Tropical zones at elevations of about 3,300 to 6,600 feet (1,000 to 2,300 m) are called montane forests. Annual precipitation is at least 79 inches (2,000 mm). These zones are created when humid air masses cool off and condense as they reach elevations of 6,600 to 9,900 feet (2,000 to 3,000 m). As the elevation increases,

Brassavola on an epiphytic branch

and the temperature decreases, the clouds become denser until they sink to the floor of the forest. If this happens at elevations between 2,600 and 5,000 feet (800 and 1,500 m), botanists call the area a cloud or monsoon forest. Because of the high humidity and the high degree of condensation, tropical mountains and montane forests are almost always shrouded in fog. Here, in the vicinity of the warm equator, between 5 and 9°N, plants reach their most prolific growth.

Temperatures are consistently 60 to 75°F (16 to 24°C). In the inner part of the forest, they vary by only 5°F (3°C). The soil often has a temperature of 71 to 73°F (22 to 23°C) and is slightly acidic. This kind of climate will last nine months of the year, sometimes even throughout the year.

The montane forest, particularly the monsoon forest, is a plant's paradise on earth. The number of epiphytes is nowhere greater. Countless species of orchids are at home in montane forests.

The *Masdevallia* orchid, an alpine epiphyte with 250 different species, is found at several different elevations in the mountain regions of Colombia, Venezuela, and Peru. Some grow in places as high as 13,000 feet (4,000 m).

In addition, the *Epidendrum*, with about 500 different species, grows in many different elevations in the tropical regions of America. Most varieties of the *Odontoglossum* are at home in the Andes. *Ada* orchids are found in the Colombian region of the Andes as well as in mountainous areas of Venezuela.

Conditions for Cultivating Orchids

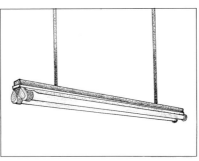

A fluorescent light fixture

Like all living things, orchids are dependent on their environment, which influences their developmental process. This is true of their natural habitat and of any home to which they are introduced.

In addition to external circumstances such as light, temperature, air and soil conditions, and nutrition, the internal, genetic predisposition of the plant plays a vital role in its development. Only favorable growing conditions make it possible for a plant to grow and to bloom.

What the orchid lover can do for the healthy growth of his plants is the subject of this chapter.

Light and Length of Day

Light is the basis for all life. This is particularly true of plant life, because light delivers the energy necessary for plant development. To assure good growing conditions for tropical orchids, it makes sense to be guided by the climatic conditions that prevail in their place of origin. That the reader's climate is totally different from that of tropics has already been established. It is different in two fundamental ways.

In the tropics, the intensity of sunlight is constant throughout the year, and the length of days is almost a constant 12 hours, plus or minus an hour.

Compared to conditions in the tropics, orchids encounter extreme conditions in other regions. In the temperate climate zones relatively long daylight hours in the summer are replaced by relatively short days during the winter. The intensity of the light in the summer is far greater than it is in winter.

Although orchids need a great deal of light, the intensity of light during temperate spring and summer months is much too strong for them. For this reason, a southern exposure is only good when the orchid can be provided with sufficient shade, such as from blinds, shades, or curtains. If shade is provided, a western location is also favorable. However, it is difficult to properly gauge the light requirements for every orchid. The leaves are good indicators of this. Tough, leatherlike, tube-shaped or round leaves indicate that the plant can tolerate relatively high-intensity light and only has to be shaded during midday. For instance, *Cymbidium*, *Vanda*, and some *Cattleya* species need a great deal of light, even an additional source of light in the evening during the winter.

21

On the other hand, orchids with very soft, limp leaves are definite shade plants, because they are very sensitive to high-intensity light. However, for some of the shade-loving plants, such as *Paphiopedilum*, the light intensity in northern temperate regions from October to March is not sufficient. These plants, too, need an additional source of light.

During the winter months in northern temperate regions all or-chids that are not in a resting period need additional artificial light. In the transitional period, it is sufficient to use artificial light to lengthen daylight hours. Orchids should not receive artificial light for more than 14 hours a day. More than that will prevent them from blooming. Experience has shown that too little light harms orchids. The plants stop growing and are unable to produce new shoots. The whole plant seems to be struggling for survival. One early warning sign is the appearance of long, weak shoots that seem to

The tube-shaped leaves of a Vanda indicate that this orchid needs high-intensity light.

grow longer than the old shoots. Indications of too much light are leaves turning light green and falling off, burn spots appearing on the leaves, and bulbs that begin to shrink in size.

Fluorescent lamps (40 or 65 watt) produce the best artificial light. A fluorescent lamp should be no farther above the orchids than 12 inches (30 cm). If this is not possible, it will be necessary to use higher-wattage bulbs.

If a high light output is needed, mercury-vapor lamps are recommended. These lights make it possible to grow orchids in a cellar.

Day and Night Temperatures

The growth of a plant is influenced by temperature. In general, it can be said that life is possible between 32 and 113°F (0 and 45°C). For tropical plants, the lower boundary might be 59°F (15°C). Below that, some plants may go into cold shock. On the other hand, leaves that receive direct sunlight are exposed to much higher temperatures and might be damaged.

The ability of a plant to absorb heat depends on its location. A plant, standing directly in front of a windowpane with no air movement, can be greatly harmed. When cultivating orchids, always be guided by the conditions in their place of origin. Orchids from the tropical or subtropical regions grow best in temperatures ranging from 63 to 82°F (17 to 28°C). Temperature extremes of 46 and 113°F (8 and 45°C)

can be tolerated by some plants, but only for a short period of time.

A thermometer is an absolute must when you introduce orchids into your environment. A thermometer that keeps track of minimum and maximum temperatures, allowing you to measure the highest and the lowest temperature over a particular time span, is best. Such a thermometer makes it possible to really know how widely the temperature varies, because it shows the highest daytime and the lowest nighttime temperatures.

Three temperature ranges (corresponding to the different climate zones in the orchid's place of origin) seem to be useful for cultivating orchids. These ranges provide cool, temperate, and warm growing conditions.

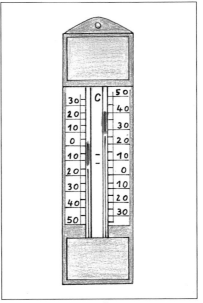

Minimum-maximum thermometer

23

Temperatures in cool greenhouses usually range from 59 to 68°F (15 to 20°C); however, with direct sun exposure (even when shaded), the temperature can rise up to 86°F (30°C). Nighttime temperatures should range between 54 and 59°F (12 and 15°C). During the winter months, daytime temperatures should be between 54 and 59°F (12 and 15°C); during the night, they should be between 46 and 68°F (8 and 20°C).

Direct sun exposure raises temperatures much higher. During the night, temperatures from between 60 and 65°F (16 and 18°C) are best.

During the winter months, daytime temperatures should be between 59 and 65°F (15 and 18°C); 55 to 59°F (13 to 15°C) should be the lower limit.

Orchids raised in heated greenhouses prefer constant temperatures. In addition, the difference in temperature between days and nights should be minimal. Daytime temperatures between 70 and 78°F (21 and 26°C) and nighttime temperatures of about 65°F (18°C) are best. These temperatures should be maintained during the winter months.

Young plants need somewhat higher temperatures. For a brief period, mature plants are able to tolerate temperatures that are less than

Odontoglossum cordatum is cultivated in a cool climate.

Phalaenopsis is a warm-climate orchid.

what is required for optimal growth.

For all three groups, nighttime temperatures should always be less than the daytime temperatures. For orchids needing cool or temperate conditions, nighttime temperatures of 40 to 43°F (4 to 6°C) are ideal for optimum growth.

Orchids thriving best in a cool climate are those from the genera *Odontoglossum* and *Zygopetalum*, some from the genus *Paphiopedilum*, and some from the genus *Cymbidium*. Those thriving best in a temperate climate are from the following genera: *Cattleya*, *Laelia*, *Oncidium*, *Stanhopea*, many *Dendrobium*, and a few *Paphiopedilum*.

Orchids thriving best in a warm climate are: *Phalaenopsis*, some from the genus *Paphiopedilum*, a few *Dendrobium*, and a few of the genus *Vanda*.

Humidity of the Air and Soil

For the purpose of this discussion, humidity is the amount of water held by the air or by the soil.

In the tropics, the relative humidity is usually between 80 and 100 percent. When the relative humidity in the air reaches 100 percent, the air is unable to absorb any more water. The higher the temperature, the more water the air can absorb. Relative humidity is measured with a hygrometer.

Many orchids can be cultivated on a windowsill, even though the humidity in the room is only 60 percent. If a windowsill is used, it is imperative to provide additional humidity, especially during the winter months when the humidity is particularly low. Use a humidifier or large bowls or dishes filled with water to increase the humidity. It is important not to set the flowerpot or

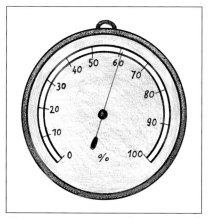

Hygrometer, an instrument for measuring relative humidity

25

any part of it directly in the water. For this reason, you may want to use upside-down saucers, which allow the pots to remain above the level of the water. Spraying the plants manually also provides additional humidity.

During the summer months, it is very important to provide sufficient humidity. The high humidity in the tropics is coupled with gentle, but constant air movement. Stagnant, heavy air is as detrimental to orchids as is a draft. It is, therefore, important to be sure that indoor locations have sufficient circulating fresh air.

Orchids preferring cool and temperate conditions do well outdoors from late spring on. However, like all other tropical and subtropical plants,

they must be brought indoors before the first frost.

Humidity in the soil is just as important for proper growth as is humidity in the air. Too much water is as harmful to a plant as is too little. A good rule of thumb is: as little as possible, but as much as necessary.

Yellowing leaves indicate the presence of too much water. If the air humidity is high, the amount of watering should be reduced. Under no circumstances should orchids be watered every day, not even during the height of the summer season. Allowing a plant a short period in which to dry out is better than drowning it.

One important difference between terrestrial and epiphytic orchids needs to be mentioned: the soil for terrestrial orchids has to be moister than does the soil for epi-

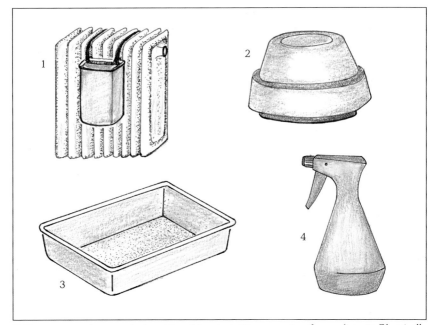

Different ways to increase the humidity of the air: 1. Water container for a radiator 2. Electrically operated humidifier 3. Water dish 4. Spray bottle

Litmus paper to check the pH value of water

phytic orchids. The roots of a terrestrial orchid should not dry out; dry soil is less damaging to epiphytes. A good rule of thumb is: water once a week in the winter and twice a week in the summer.

Water Used for Watering Orchids

The quality of the water used for watering is also important. Tap water is usually not suitable. Water used for watering or spraying orchids should be soft, low in sodium, and free of chlorine. The pH value should be 7, or the growth of the plant will be negatively affected. Chlorine can

Oxygenating water with the help of an electric fish-tank pump

be partially removed from tap water by letting the water stand in a container for several days. The chlorine will evaporate. The water can be softened by boiling it.

Rainwater is usually soft and can be used providing it does not contain damaging particles (for instance, water that runs off a tar roof or rainwater from industrial regions). Since clean rainwater is slightly acidic, it is very good for orchids. However, it must not be too acidic. A pH value of 5 to 5.5 is best for watering orchids. It is easy to measure the pH value with litmus paper. If the rainwater is too acidic, it can be diluted with tap water until the proper pH value is established.

Tap water can be made acidic with untreated peat moss. Fill a small cheesecloth with the moss and submerge it in the watering can until the desired pH value is reached.

Nurseries sell tablets to decalcify water. Water to be used on orchids should always be at room temperature. In addition, the oxygen content of the water is important for orchids. Water that has been in a water can for several days is usually low in oxygen. A water pump, such as the kind used in a fish aquarium, is ideal for oxygenating water. However, vigorous stirring will do just as well.

Growth and Development

The growth and flowering of a plant takes place in rhythmic periods which are influenced by internal and external factors that act on each other.

For example, an external factor, such as lowering the temperature, can activate an internal factor, such as initiating or influencing a plant's rest period. The change from active growth to rest period, nevertheless, is genetically determined and can only be marginally influenced or altered.

Almost all orchids grow in an observable pattern. First, a shoot and a leaf appear. These are followed by the flower. A totally uniform rate seldom occurs in nature; it can only be accomplished with young plants that are brought to the flowering stage under very controlled circumstances.

Growth is increased by raising the temperature; it is inhibited by reducing it. In reverse, raising the temperature stops the rest period; lowering the temperature initiates the rest period. The degree of humidity in the air can support this cause-and-effect process. In fact, the climate is a very important factor in the biological rhythm of a plant.

Another factor is the movement of the sun, which also influences the way precipitation takes place in the tropics. That, in turn, influences orchids. Accustomed to a rather steady weather pattern in the tropics, orchids develop a certain growth pattern of the main stem, as is the case with *Phalaenopsis* and *Vanda*. It seems that only slight changes in temperature and amounts of light cause changes in the rate of growth.

The dependency of growth and the development of flowers on the number of daylight hours was given too much importance in the past. Temperature and humidity play a much larger role—as long as the daylight hours are not shortened or lengthened to any great degree. Even the differences in daily temperature and humidity in an orchid's place of origin play a greater role than the length of daylight.

In temperate zones, however, the length of daylight does play a role. *Cattleya*, for instance, can be prevented from going into its rest period by adding a moderate amount of additional light (100 lux). On the other hand, the growth period can be ended by reducing the available light. Here, a change in the timetable takes place. Manipulating the periods of available light does not initiate growth in flowers. However, since only a limited number of specific experiments have been done, we do not know enough about this subject.

Great differences in temperature cause growth and rest periods. The effects of these temperature changes are most clearly observable in *Cymbidium* orchids. Flower production begins when daytime temperatures are about 68°F (20°C) and nighttime temperatures are around 50 to 57°F (10 to 14°C). *Phalaenopsis schilleriana* and its hybrids will only bloom when the nighttime temperature is under 68°F (20°C) for at least 2 or 3 weeks. Otherwise, the plant produces offshoots, commonly called "keikis."

28

Phalaenopsis hybrid

Potting Materials and Repotting

The potting material or substrate must allow air and water to move through it. At the same time, the material has to retain moisture and nutrients.

All natural substrates can be used: dried fern roots, peat moss, and shredded bark. People also use artificial chips, artificial fibers, perlite of different origins, sandy loam, charcoal, and fall leaves. If only a few plants have to be repotted, it is best to buy commercial, premixed substrates. If you want to make your own mix, the following are well-tested recipes.

29

Potting Mix 1
(Fern root as base)

3 parts fern root
3 parts fibrous moss
3 parts of rigid plastic foam beads
1 part charcoal, approximately ⅒ to
⅓ inch (3–8 mm) in diameter
   For epiphytes, additional fern root and plastic foam particles can be added in order to make this base more porous, increasing the flow of air and water. For terrestrial orchids, replace the fibrous moss with sandy loam or peat moss. For lady's slipper, (*Paphiopedilum*) add a teaspoon (2 g) of calcium carbonate to each 2 quarts (2 l) of substrate.

Potting Mix 2
(Peat moss as base)

3 parts peat moss
3 parts pumice stone
3 parts of rigid plastic foam beads
1 part charcoal

Add 1 teaspoon (2 g) of calcium carbonate for each quart (litre) of potting mix. Peat moss is ideal for *Phalaenopsis, Oncidium,* and *Lycaste*.

Potting Mix 3
(Fir bark as base)

5 parts fir bark (small bark chips for orchids)
2 parts pumice stone
2 parts peat moss
1 part charcoal
1 tsp (2 g) calcium carbonate for each quart (litre) of potting soil
   This substrate is ideal for epiphytes that are grown in flower pots.

Potting Mix 4
(Lumpy, commercial peat moss as base)

1 part lumpy peat moss
1 part rigid plastic foam beads

30

This mix is particularly suited for *Phalaenopsis* grown in flower pots. Use peat moss to which a small amount of trace minerals has been added.

Fertilizer added to mixes 1 through 4

In general, plants receive sufficient amounts of basic nutrients; however, they often lack certain trace elements. This can be prevented by adding a commercial plant fertilizer consisting of trace minerals, such as iron, copper, manganese, zinc, molybdenum, boron, and magnesium in balanced proportions.

Be sure to follow the directions on the label.

Potting Mix 5
(Orchid chips)

Orchid chips are beads or chips made by a special process that uses steam. The surface of the beads or chips is rough. All kinds of orchids can be grown in this mix. It has the following advantages:
• It is consistent in mixture and structure.
• Water uniformly adheres to its surface, making it easily available to the plant.
• The availability of air is constant. Excess water drains off and root bulbs remain moist.

• Hard water does not leave deposits on roots or the mix. Overfertilizing is not possible.

Tips for watering when using orchid chips

As far as watering is concerned, nighttime temperatures are more important than are daytime temperatures. If the location of the orchid has a relative humidity of 50 to 80 percent, the following applies:

Orchids grown in cool to temperate climates

Summer: nights from 59 to 64°F (15 to 18°C); winter: nights from 46 to 54°F (8 to 12°C); water thoroughly every third to fourth day.

Orchids grown in temperate to warm climates

Summer: nights from 61 to 75°F (16 to 24°C); winter: nights from 59 to 64°F (15 to 18°C); water thoroughly every second to third day.

When growing orchids in winter in orchid-chip mix, you will need to add a special food or fertilizer to the water used for watering once every week. Check your local grower or nursery for recommendations.

Repotting

Orchids should be repotted whenever the substrate has deteriorated, or when plant roots do not have a sufficient amount of air available. Repotting is also needed when the plant outgrows the pot and new shoots do not have enough room to grow. New shoots growing over the edge of the pot usually break off very

31

easily, and the plant sustains considerable damage when this happens.

It is best to repot when new growth begins; in other words, when new shoots and new roots begin to appear. This can usually be observed around the middle or the end of January. Depending on the kind of orchid, or if conditions are not quite right, repotting can be done later. For instance, if the plant is being kept in a cooler environment and is watered sparingly, active growth can be delayed.

The best time to repot, with few exceptions, is between the end of January and the end of May.

For *Phalaenopsis*, August is also a good time, but here, too, repotting is possible between February and September.

Orchids that have pseudobulbs, such as *Cattleya, Laelia, Dendrobium, Odontoglossum, Oncidium, Cymbidium* and all their relatives, can be repotted even when their shoots are

2 inches (5 cm) tall. However, the earlier, the better!

Before being repotted, the plant must have at least two to three pseudobulbs. The remaining, older bulbs are called "back bulbs." They can be made to produce new shoots. However, such plants usually need a longer rest period in order to look presentable and to begin blooming again.

The size of the pot should be large enough so that the plant can continue to grow for as long as the potting mixture lasts. Containers that are too large permit too much moisture to remain in the mixture. The roots begin to rot, and not enough air reaches the root system.

Settle on a pot that's just slightly larger than the old one. It's wise to check the moisture content of the mixture.

When repotting, remove the plant carefully from the old pot without damaging the roots. Shake the root system slightly. It's best if the root system doesn't break apart. Sick or damaged roots should be removed

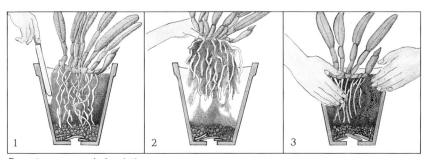

Repotting a sympodial orchid
1. The roots are carefully loosened from the side of the old pot and the plant is removed.
2. The old substrate is carefully shaken off; sick or damaged root parts are removed, as well as dried portions of bulb; and if desired, the plant is divided.
3. The oldest bulb is always positioned towards the edge of the pot; hollow spaces between the roots are filled in with the new mixture; the mixture is pressed down firmly enough for the plant to stand securely in the new pot.

carefully. Use a smooth cut with sharp scissors. This is the point where a plant may be divided. Fill one-third of the new pot with a loose material (pieces of a broken pot, plastic foam beads, or something similar). Next, fill in the root system with the new substrate and put the plant on top of the drainage material already in the pot.

Hold the plant in position so that the base of the plant is at the same height as the edge of the pot. The oldest bulb is always closest to the edge of the pot. With the help of a wooden stick, carefully fill in the rest of the hollow spaces. pressing the substrate firmly enough for the plant to be held securely in place. Fill in up to ⅓ inch (1 cm) of the edge of the pot. Additional mix should be

added in case the root ball becomes loose, but care should be taken not to damage the roots.

Monopodial plants, such as *Vanda*, *Renanthera*, and *Phalaenopsis*, are placed in the center of the new pot. This rule also applies to *Paphiopedilum*.

During the day, the plant may be sprayed with water to support good growth. At night, the humidity in the air is higher anyway, due to the lower temperature. The plant should not be watered during the first two or three weeks. Initially, the plant should be kept in the shade. The plant needs to have the temperature raised by 10 to 15°F (5 to 10°C).

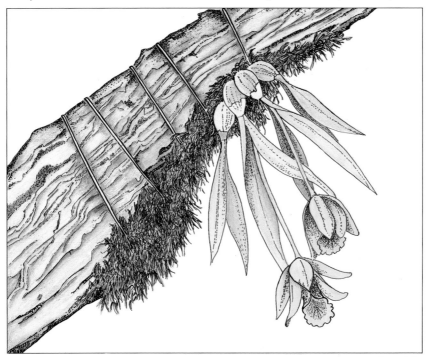

Epiphytes are only covered with a small amount of potting mixture and tied to a piece of wood; for example, to a rootstock.

33

Paphiopedilum may be watered after 8 to 10 days. However, the leaves should be sprayed frequently after repotting; this is especially important for the leaves of these orchids.

Calanthe and *Dendrobium phalaenopsis* and their hybrids should be repotted every year.

Depending on the type of potting mixture used, *Paphiopedilum* and *Phalaenopsis* are repotted only every two to three years.

For sympodial orchids, such as *Cattleya, Laelia, Oncidium, Odontoglossum*, and *Cymbidium*, repotting is only necessary every two years. Repotting can even be delayed until the plant outgrows its pot or the mixture is used up. Monopodial orchids such as *Vanda, Renanthera*, and their relatives and hybrids should not be repotted more frequently than every three years. When repotting, the leafless portion of the shoot is cut off.

Tree-dwelling orchids are less likely to need attention. When necessary, the root bulb is covered with a small amount of new substrate and retied to its support (which may be a piece of bark, a block of fern roots, a piece of rootstock, or a branch). Use noncorroding wire, artificial ties, or strings cut from old nylon stockings to tie the orchid to its support. A dry period is not necessary with these orchids. When the plant is generously sprayed, it will very quickly show new growth.

Propagation of Orchids

Sooner or later, most orchid growers want to increase the number of their orchids. This can be done in several different ways.

The usual way to propagate plants at home is to use seeds. This is called generative or sexual reproduction. Through fertilization, a new generation is created. In contrast, the vegetative process of propagation is a nonsexual process. Here, the plant is divided, shoots are rooted, or runners are separated from the mother plant, and so forth.

Sadly, the propagation of orchids is not that simple.

Generative Propagation

In the case of orchids, it is difficult to propagate using seeds. Because the orchid seed does not have nutritional tissue, the plant must rely on a particular fungus in the soil. Part of the fungus grows into the seed tissue of the orchid and supplies nourishment to the young seedling. The seed capsule must be taken off the plant no later than the moment when the seams of the capsule begin to open up. It is better to harvest the capsule when it is still green, just when the tips begin to turn brown.

The exact time when a capsule is ripe differs even within the same genus. Observation is all that can be offered as a guideline for when to harvest.

The seeds should be sown close to the mother plant, in an evenly moist, moss-covered surface. It will take months before the first one or two seedling leaves are visible, and then, only with a magnifying glass. The first roots appear even later.

There are special substrates available which include all the nutrition orchid seeds need. Young seedlings do not have to depend on a fungus. Different powdered substrates for propagation are available. Besides a gelatinlike carbohydrate, which serves as an anchor for the seeds, these substrates contain mineral nutrients, growth hormones, and vitamins. It is important to work under sterile conditions in order to avoid contamination by airborne bacteria. Sterile conditions are easily achieved by positioning the container with the substrate over a pot of steaming water or by putting the substrate in a glass-covered, sterile container. All implements needed for this process are available in specialty stores. Often, it is necessary to transplant young seedlings to a different substrate under sterile conditions. These precautions are usually necessary until the young plants are one or two years old and are ready to be transplanted into a substrate that should not be too coarse. This work is exciting for an orchid lover.

Vegetative Propagation

Increasing the number of orchids by division is much easier for the beginner and has a much greater chance of success. The best time to divide a plant is at the time of repotting. Often, plants that already have developed more than one main root stem separate naturally. It is important to make sure that each portion is securely anchored in the new substrate. In the beginning it is often necessary to support the plant with a U-shaped wire. In addition, the new plant has to have sufficient space for its roots in the new pot (see

When repotting orchids that grow in rosette-like fashion, the roots usually separate naturally, dividing the plant into two parts.

In the case of single-stem orchids, the top portion of the plant that has developed air roots can be used for further cultivation.

page 32). Each plant to be divided must consist of three shoots that have developed in the last three years. If this rule is not observed, the plant is seriously weakened, and it may be years before it will bloom. A plant that is to be divided, such as a *Paphiopedilum* or similar orchids, must consist of at least six shoots.

35

Use a sharp knife and cover the cut surface of each new plant with sawdust to avoid infecting the plant. The same procedure should be followed for sympodial orchids. Each portion should have at least three leaves on each bulb. Bulbs without leaves, such as those from *Cattleya* and *Laelia*, are best discarded. Only leafless bulbs from the *Cymbidium* orchid can be successfully divided, if they are healthy and have not begun to shrink.

Insert only the lower half of the new bulb in peat moss to encourage the developing bud to grow. As soon as the new shoot is at least as big as the bulb, the plant can be potted in the appropriate substrate. The new roots will begin to grow at this point. However, it will take several years for the new plant to bloom. Orchids with bulblike shoots, such as *Dendrobium* and *Epidendrum*, can develop scions at these shoots. To initiate this, the bulblike shoot, without leaves if possible, is planted horizontally in peat moss and kept in a container at even temperatures and humidity. After a few weeks, when scions have developed small leaves and new roots, the young plants can be carefully removed from the stem and planted in small pots. They will continue to need a uniform temperature and humidity.

In the case of orchids with monopodial growth, such as *Vanda*, *Ascocentrum*, and *Renanthera*, the upper portion can be used for further cultivation. The portion that will make up the new plant, however, should be at least 8 inches (20 cm) high. The normal blooming rhythm will not be interrupted. The lower portion of the plant usually develops a new shoot from the uppermost bud that lies opposite the earlier flower.

With *Phalaenopsis*, the development of new buds can be initiated at the flower stem. At the beginning of summer, the days get longer and nighttime temperatures remain above 68°F (20°C) for a couple of weeks. In some species and their hybrids, this causes flower buds to change and become small shoot buds. These little plants, called "keikeis" in Hawaii, soon develop leaves and roots. They can be taken off the mother plant in the fall and treated as new plants. This process can also be initiated at the flower stem by using a root-building substance (sold in specialty stores).

Nutrition and Nutritional Needs

For the longest time, orchid growers debated whether or not orchids need to be fertilized. Eventually, it was agreed that orchids grow much better when the plant receives fertilizer. A proper feeding schedule that takes the growing requirements into consideration produces richer-blooming orchids. Nevertheless, a few rules must be observed.

Synthetic substrates with their poor nutritional value make feeding orchids almost a necessity. However, caution is required because orchids do not tolerate normal concentrations of fertilizers. It is important to dilute fertilizers or to buy a commercial fertilizer specially prepared for orchids. The same amount of fertilizer should not be given throughout the year. Growth and rest periods should be observed, and feeding should be suspended during the latter. It is best to fertilize once a week from February to April and from September through October; twice-weekly applications are used from May to the end of August.

The most important nutritional substances are already contained in orchid food available in specialty stores. Nitrogen (N) supports the growth of the plant; phosphorus (P) influences the development of the flowers; and potassium (K) strengthens and supports the developing flowers. Other substances necessary for healthy growth, such as trace elements, are also included in ready-to-use products. Some mixes of fertilizer are geared to increase growth; others are used to increase flowering. The concentration of the main nutrients is usually given in a number, such as: N:P:K = 20:5:10.

It is also possible to use an or-

ganic fertilizer. However, the nutrients in organic fertilizers take longer to become usable than the water-soluble salts in chemical fertilizers.

Diseases, Parasites, and Their Treatments

Unfortunately, orchids are always being attacked by parasites. Less severe infections are usually harmless. Washing the plant with a soapy solution is as effective as using a chemically produced product (many parasites develop a resistance to these over time). Adding a nicotine solution to the water is very effective. Spraying regularly (once a month) with a substance that is absorbed by the roots will protect most plants against harmful insects. This treatment, however, is limited to orchids grown in the house. The instructions on the label should always be closely followed.

Red spider mites are very common and hard to eliminate. Red spi-

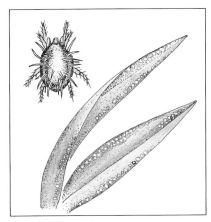

Red spider mite

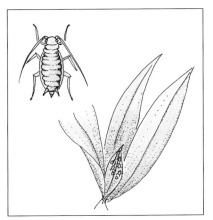

Aphid

37

der mites usually are a problem when the temperature is too high and the humidity too low. Leaves that appear to have been sprinkled with a whitish substance or are turning yellow are usually a sure sign of red spider mites; in the advanced stage, the leaves will drop off.

Start by thoroughly washing the leaves. If the infection is severe, use an appropriate systemic product. Treat the infected plant for 8 to 10 days at a time, and repeat the treatment three or four times. Treating the plant with a nicotine solution is also helpful.

Aphids suck plant juices from the leaves and transfer viral infections. They prefer to suck on young leaves and flower buds. After an infection, the leaves and stems become weak, and flower buds don't open. The best remedy is to wash the plant with a soapy solution. In case of a severe infection, a systemic solution should be used.

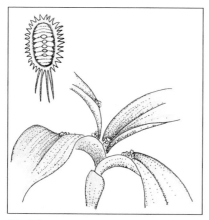

Mealybug

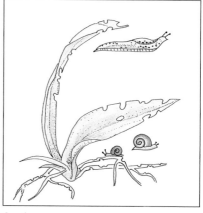

Snail

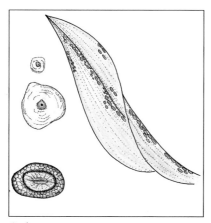

Scale

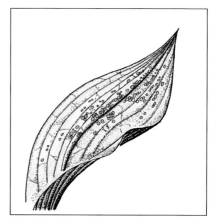

Viral infection

Black rot

Mealybugs attack many orchids. They are visible as sticky, cottonlike spots that usually appear at points of juncture, such as the crook between two leaves. Afflicted plants usually look weak and shrivelled. If only a few places are infected, touch those places with a cotton swab dipped in denatured alcohol. If the infection is more widespread, the plant should be treated with a systemic pesticide.

Scales are found on pseudobulbs and leaves. They are round or oval shell-like parasites that cause leaves to turn yellow. Use the same treatment as you would for mealybugs.

Snails are attracted to greenhouses because they like warm, humid climates. They attack every part of the plant and leave visible holes in the leaves. Snails leave behind slimy trails. Commercially available pesticides work well, especially those in liquid form, because they reach snails that may be hiding.

Viral infections are present when leaves show yellow and black mottling or stripes. The flowers are also affected. Many different virus strains destroy plant tissue. Viral infections are transferred from one plant to another. The caregiver comes in contact with the tissues or the sap of an infected plant and passes it on to another plant. Sadly, there is no cure for a viral disease. An infected plant must be disposed of in the trash.

Black rot is caused by several different fungi that thrive particularly well in a climate with low temperatures and high humidity. The presence of this disease becomes obvious with the appearance of characteristic reddish spots with yellow outlines. The disease spreads from the leaves downwards and from the bulbs and rhizomes upwards. Infected parts of a plant should be removed and destroyed. The whole plant needs to be treated with a fungicide. Severely infected plants are best destroyed.

The best protection against diseases and parasites is always a clean, well-ventilated (but not too drafty) environment in which all the necessary conditions for healthy growth are provided. In order to prevent an infection from getting out of hand, inspect plants carefully with a magnifying glass and consider getting advice from a specialist. All instruments and tools used to treat an infected plant must be thoroughly sterilized, and all diseased plants and substrates should be destroyed.

39

Where Can Orchids Be Cultivated?

Most people will agree that orchids make good houseplants. Orchids can be cultivated just like any other houseplant if proper choices are made.

The major difficulty is the central heating systems in our homes. Rooms where the air is too warm and too dry are often a problem. But the orchid lover has several means to address these problems.

Many technical aids make caring for orchids rather easy. Of course, for the serious orchid lover, a small greenhouse would be ideal, because it makes it possible to provide the necessary high humidity as well as warm temperatures.

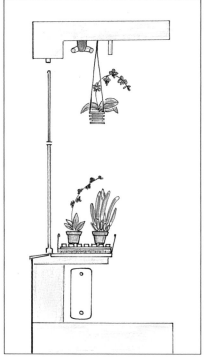

Orchids growing on a windowsill

In order to increase humidity, flowerpots turned upside down in a water-filled container are used as a platform for orchids.

The Windowsill

The cultivation of orchids usually begins on a windowsill. The most important consideration is the location of the window. A southern exposure provides a plant with maximum light but very high temperatures. A window that faces south can only be recommended when either a shade or a blind can provide the necessary shade.

Windows with eastern or western exposures are best. However, on hot summer days, shade must be provided for windows with western exposures. For some species, a window that faces north is also suitable.

The width of the windowsill should be at least 8 to 10 inches (20 to 25 cm). Louvred blinds that provide shade are always recommended.

If the windowsill sits directly above a radiator, it is imperative that a water container be provided. In addition, a container filled with water should also be placed on the windowsill. Flowerpots turned upside down and placed in the container serve as an ideal place to stand other flowerpots. The water in the container must always be filled. The evaporating water will create 100 percent relative humidity!

A plastic heating cable under the container keeps the water warm and encourages evaporation. A layer of gravel on the bottom of the container can also be very helpful.

Spraying the plants directly with water is also a good method to encourage growth and to assure the well-being of the orchid. Air movement is helpful for good growth; usually, a regular airing of the room is sufficient. However, a draft must

Enclosed flower window with vents

be avoided at all costs!

During the winter, additional artificial lighting is necessary. Orchid plants need 12 hours of light. Depending on the location of the window, the following orchids and hybrids are suitable.

1. **Southern exposure** (where shade can be provided): *Cattleya* hybrids, *Cymbidium traceyanum* and *C. lowianum*, mini *Cymbidium*, *Dendrobium chrysotoxum*, *D. nobile*, and *D.* hybrids, *Laelia anceps*, *L. autumnalis*, *Lycaste virginalis*, *Odontoglossum bictoniense*, *O. grande*, *O. uro-skinneri*, *Oncidium varicosum*.

2. **Southeastern, southern, and southwestern exposures** of

41

even temperatures and a minimum of 59°F (15°C): *Aërides odoratum, Cattleya* varieties and hybrids, *Laelia* varieties and hybrids, *Paphiopedilum* varieties and hybrids, *Phalaenopsis* varieties and hybrids, *Rhynchostylis,* and *Vanda.*

3. **Eastern, northeastern, north-western, and western exposures:** *Coelogne, Epidendrum* varieties, *Masdevallia, Maxillaria,*

A glass cabinet should always have an additional source of light, a thermometer, and a hygrometer.

Odontoglossum, Oncidium, Paphiopedilum fairieanum, P. insigne, P. venustum, P. villosum, and *P.* hybrids originating in cooler climates.

The Flower Window

A so-called flower window is a wonderful solution for cultivating orchids. The window extends to the outside and is separated from the rest of the room by a glass sliding panel, providing more even humidity for the plants. While the humidity can be easily controlled, establishing proper temperatures (particularly during the winter) is a problem. However, temperatures can be regulated with a thermostatically controlled heating device. Of course, no additional heating is required if there is a radiator under the windowsill.

The availability of fresh air inside the enclosure is important. During the warm season, fresh air can be brought in from the outside. Orchids grown in such a window also need an additional source of light.

Orchids that are suitable for a flower window are much more numerous than are those for a windowsill. However, the condition of light always has to be considered. Usually, light from above the plant is lacking and needs to be provided. Here are a few orchids and hybrids that are suitable for such a window: *Phalaenopsis* varieties and hybrids, *Laelia, Brassavola, Brassia, Cattleya* varieties, *Maxillaria, Oncidium, Epidendrum, Encyclia* varieties and hybrids, and *Paphiopedilum* varieties that love a warm climate.

An indoor display case

Glass Cabinet or Glass Display Case

Glass cabinets are very decorative and often become the special jewel of a living room. Different constructions that are aesthetically beautiful and useful are available. The exact location for a cabinet or display case is usually chosen from an interior-decorating point of view. Thus, cultivating orchids, not just bringing them into bloom, takes a bit of experience, because sufficient light is often lacking. If natural light is poor, additional artificial light has to be provided. For very light-hungry plants, it might be necessary to in-

43

stall mercury-vapor lamps. A hygrometer and a thermometer will be very useful. A glass cabinet is best for orchids that do not have particularly great lighting requirements; otherwise, the need for artificial light is too great.

Phalaenopsis and its varieties have proved to be particularly suited for glass cabinets. With additional lighting, warmth-loving species, such as *Paphiopedilum, Oncidium,* and their relatives are also recommended, as well as orchids that are cultivated in a flower window (see page 43).

Sun-room

Often a sun-room or a veranda can be a good place for orchids. Because these areas are open to the living room, additional heat is not necessary, providing that the right kind of orchids are chosen. If warmth-loving orchids are cultivated, an additional source of heat might be required. In any case, it is important to provide sufficient ventilation.

Since these plants usually receive overhead light, a sun-room is an ideal place for growing orchids. However, an additional light in the winter always makes sense.

Humidity is usually not a problem. A sun-room offers many possibilities to provide the necessary humidity in the air. Any orchid that is cultivated indoors can be placed in a sun-room—which gives the gardener a wide variety of choices.

Small Greenhouse

Without a doubt, the ultimate for every orchid lover is a small greenhouse, divided into cool, temperate, and warm zones. The larger the air space, the easier it is to establish a good climate. Conditions in such a controlled environment are ideal.

When building a greenhouse, it is important to plan the orientation so that you will have the proper exposure. In the past, a north-south expo-

Small greenhouse for cultivating orchids

sure was preferred. Today, the tendency is to choose an east-west exposure. A north-south orientation allows the best use of the light, but with an east-west exposure the intensity of light and the temperature differs within the room, allowing you to cultivate plants with different needs. Tables and stairlike structures permit the maximum use of space. It is often possible to install three to four levels of shelves. In addition, epiphytes can be grown on wires strung alongside the glass walls.

Heating, a water source, shades, and additional, artificial light are variables that can be controlled in order to provide a perfect environment for an orchid culture.

The Basement

Even in the basement or other similarly dark places, orchid cultivation is possible when fluorescent lighting and mercury-vapor lamps are provided. A basement might even provide ideal conditions because it is usually consistently cool and humid. Often, no additional heating is necessary. However, it is important to provide good ventilation and, of course, artificial light.

The amount of light depends on the size of the surface over which the orchids are spread out. A good rule of thumb for orchid cultivation is: 100 to 400 watts of electric light for each square yard (m) of surface. It is important to have the electrical fixtures installed by professionals in order to avoid hazardous conditions. The floor should be insulated against moisture and water.

What to Look For When Buying Orchids

There is no such thing as a beginner's orchid. A beginner should start with plants that are easy to care for.

It is important to be clear about the climate (cool, temperate, or warm) in your house. What kind of orchid should you start with? It is wise to seek the advice of a specialist. No doubt you will be introduced to a variety of easy-to-care-for orchids.

It always makes sense to buy mature plants. Young plants are usually less expensive, but they are also much more sensitive. Following this advice will save a lot of disappointment. In addition, it is advisable in the beginning to get detailed information from an orchid association.

What follow are a few orchids a beginner might consider: *Cattleya* and its hybrids, *Cymbidium* and miniature *Cymbidium*, *Dendrobium* and its hybrids, *Phalaenopsis* and its hybrids, *Odontoglossum*, *Oncidium* and its relatives and hybrids.

The following are suitable for those who already have a little experience: *Ascocentrum*, *Bifrenaria*, *Brassia*, *Calanthe*, *Leptotes*, *Lycaste*, *Maxillaria*, *Miltonia*, *Renanthera*, *Sophronitis*, *Vanda*, *Zygopetalum*; in addition, *Ascocendra*, *Vuylstekeara*, and *Wilsonara*.

45

Orchids as Potted Plants

Orchids are very popular as potted plants. There are a number of orchids that are recommended for the beginner. The following belong to this category: *Phalaenopsis* varieties and hybrids, *Paphiopedilum* varieties and hybrids, *Odontoglossum*, its relatives and hybrids, and many more.

For the more experienced, the following orchids are recommended: *Miltonia*, *Vanda*, and *Zygopetalum*.

All orchids discussed in this chapter are recommended for cultivation and are easy to care for. They are listed according to their requirements for specific location and care.

Easy-to-Cultivate Genera, Species, and Hybrids

Phalaenopsis

Phalaenopsis, also called the Malaysian flower, is at home in Bangladesh, south China, Thailand, Vietnam, in the Philippines, New Guinea, and in the tropical, northern region of Australia. The 400 species grow at elevations of 300 to 1,300 feet (100 to 400 m), which means they need lots of warmth and high humidity. They usually grow as epiphytes on trees at the edges of tropical or monsoon forests, protected from direct sunlight by the leaves of the trees. A few also grow on rocks as lithophytes.

Phalaenopsis have fleshy, wide leaves with thick, strong roots and short or long, trailing flower stalks that develop from the axis of the leaves.

Phalaenopsis

The large, colorful flowers with their three-lobed lips are very conspicuous. These are perfect plants for the beginner.

Conditions for cultivation

Phalaenopsis belongs to the group of orchids that need warm temperatures. Temperatures should not fall below 64°F (18°C) at night and not go beyond 77°F (25°C) during the day. If the humidity is high, and the plant has absorbed sufficient water, it will be able to tolerate 86°F (30°C). If the outside temperature is very high, the plant needs to be shaded. Since this plant needs high temperatures, it is difficult to maintain sufficient humidity in the air. Humidity must, therefore, be constantly monitored. If possible, keep freshly potted plants in a 100 percent relative humidity until they have developed new roots.

Phalaenopsis does not like direct sunlight. Twelve hours of daylight (about 400 lux) is ideal. The leaves should neither be dark green (shadow leaves), nor yellowish green (sun leaves); rather they should have a medium green color with a light grey shimmer. Because *Phalaenopsis* cannot store water, it must have water constantly available. The amount of water needed and the number of waterings depend on the substrate or potting mixture. Orchids potted in orchid chips and bark compost need frequent waterings; fern-root substrate holds moisture longer. Peat moss retains extra water much longer than other materials. Instead of watering the plant, you can set the flowerpot in a water bath and allow the plant to absorb the moisture it

needs. A plant kept year-round in half shade and watered liberally requires less water in the winter, assuring good flower production. *Phalaenopsis* orchids are not very demanding (see the chapter on "Potting Materials and Repotting"). The most frequent pests are red spider mites and thrips.

Typical problems and their causes

- Root rot: Too much water. Root bulbs must dry out between waterings.
- Plant does not grow and the leaves are limp: Too little water or the temperature is too cool. It is also possible that the plant has been repotted at the wrong time. Repotting should take place when new roots are just beginning to develop.
- Root tips are dry while the root bulb itself is still wet: Too much fertilizer.
- Burn spots on leaves: Plant is exposed to too much direct sunlight.
- Limp leaves with a wilted look: Not enough humidity. The plant, roots and all, should be submerged in warm water.

Results of successful cultivation

- Plant has a good root system.
- The leaves are medium green and strong. Each new leaf has the same size as the previous one.
- A three to five-year-old plant has four to six leaves that are up to 24 inches (60 cm) long and 10 inches

(25 cm) wide. The plant is strong enough to support a large blooming.

• Blooming will continue for about two to three months. When it is finished, remove the flower about 1 inch (2 to 3 cm) above the next lower "eye." From this eye, the plant produces a new bloom. Cutting the old flower will double the flowering period. If flowers are removed at the end of the summer season, the eye will produce new plant shoots instead of new flowers, acting as a kind of vegetative propagation.

• In general, it takes about two years for a new plant to get used to a new location. For that reason, it is important to observe the direction in which the plant is growing. A plant should only be repotted if the substrate is used up or if the pot has become too small.

• Hybrids are preferred by most orchid lovers over natural plants because of their strong growth and willingness to produce rich flowers. Freshly repotted plants require special attention. They need 100 percent relative humidity until they have developed new roots.

Phalaenopsis cornu-cervi

Recommended Phalaenopsis varieties

Phalaenopsis amabilis
Usually four leaves, the flowering area may be up to 32 inches (80 cm) long with limited branching, and up to 5 inches (12 cm) wide; overall color is white.
Home: From Malaysia to New Guinea, the Philippines, and northwest Australia.
Blooms from October to July (also all year round).

Phalaenopsis cornu-cervi
Four to six leaves; blossoms are 1½ to 2 inches (4 to 5 cm) in diameter; flowers are yellow to yellow green with red brown spots; grows as an epiphyte on trees at elevations of 1,000 feet (300 m).
Home: Sikkim, Burma, Thailand, Sumatra, Java, Borneo.
Blooms from April to October (also year-round).

Phalaenopsis equestris
Four to six leaves; flowers grow upright to a diameter of 1 inch (3 cm); color is gentle pink with red brown to carmine violet spots.
Home: The Philippines and Taiwan at elevations beginning at 1,000 feet (300 m).
Blooms from May to October (all year round).

Phalaenopsis lueddemanniana
Six to eight leaves; flower stalks up to 20 inches (50 cm) long; grows over several years; flowers, up to 2 inches (5 cm) in diameter; pink to cream in color with carmine spots.
Home: The Philippines.

Blooms from April till October.

Phalaenopsis mannii
Six leaves; floral axes up to 8 inches (20 cm) long; diameter of flowers about 2 inches (5 cm); yellowish green with brown spots.
Home: Himalayas (Sikkim to Vietnam); epiphyte at elevations up to 2,600 feet (800 m).
Blooms from March to July.

Phalaenopsis mariae
Four to six leaves; branched floral axes; up to 16 inches (40 cm) and 1½ inches (4 cm) in diameter; white with strong red brown spots; flower markings vary widely.
Home: The Philippines and Borneo, at elevations of 2,300 feet (700 m).
Blooms from June to September.

Phalaenopsis sanderiana
Four to six leaves; floral axes up to 36

Phalaenopsis stuartiana

49

inches (90 cm) long; flowers up to 4 inches (10 cm) in diameter; pink and carmine in color.
Home: The Philippines.
Blooms from December to July.

Phalaenopsis schilleriana
Four to six leaves; leaves are 13×5 inches $(35 \times 12$ cm), brown green with silver speckles; numerous, branched floral axes, some up to 30 inches (80 cm) long; flowers are 2½ to 3 inches (7 cm) in diameter; pink with carmine red markings.
Home: The Philippines, at elevations around 1,000 to 1,300 feet (300 to 400 m).
Blooms from November to March.

Phalaenopsis stuartiana
Four to six leaves; leaves are elongated and elliptically shaped, dark green, horizontally striped, and speckled; flower stalks up to 32 inches (80 cm) long, branched and produce numerous flowers; flowers are up to 2¼ inches (6 cm) in diameter; white and yellowish orange

Phalaenopsis Golden Sands

with speckles.
Home: The Philippines.
Blooms from November till March.

Phalaenopsis sumatrana
Four to six leaves; leaves are 8×4 inches $(20 \times 10$ cm), fresh green, pointed; flower stems up to 8 inches (20 cm) long continue to grow for some time, followed by more flowering; flowers are round, 2 inches (5 cm) in diameter; green yellow with carmine red speckles.
Home: Southern Thailand, Malaysia, Sumatra, Java, and Borneo; can live as an epiphyte near water, at

Phalaenopsis equestris was one of the parents of the first Phalaenopsis hybrid.

New Hybrids

Phal. Bernstein (Barbara Mohler × Mambo)
Primrose yellow, poppy red, and striped; lip has the same color as the markings.

Phal. Corina (Suemid coringiana)
Yellow, primrose stripes.

Phal. Deventerana (amabilis × amboinensis)
Yellow with red dots.

Phal. Gabriel Schumacher (Mad Hatter × violacea)
Yellow; sepals and petals have a reddish tint; lip is primrose red.

Phal. Golden Sands (Fenton Davis Avant × lueddemanniana)
Sunflower yellow, faint red speckles; lip has the same color.

Phal. Ines Dankmeyer (Mad Hatter × Initial)
Red with dark stripes.

Phal. Kochs Schneestern (Long Life × Schöne von Unna)
Yellow with red stripes.

Phal. Kurt Haussermann (Mad Lips × violacea)
White, primrose red veins; lip primrose red and orange.

Phal. Lieselotte (Mildred's Baby × lueddemanniana)
Red with fine dots.

Phal. Little Kris (Cassandra × Pink Minuet)
White with red dots.

Phal. Long Life 'Unna' (Orchid Acres × Fairway Pack)
Clone with white base and light yellow lip.

Phalaenopsis mariae

51

New Hybrids (continued)

Phal. Marquise (Lady Ruby × Redfan)
White to light carnation red; dark stripes of the same color.
Phal. Mildred's Baby (Mildred Karleen × Opaline)
Pure white with primrose red lip.
Phal. Parade (Vallauris × Marquise)
Yellow with red veins.
Phal. Polo (Redfan × javanica)
White with primrose red markings; lip in the color of the markings.
Phal. Redwine (Estrellita × lueddemanniana)
Red flower; white column with yellow edges.
Phal. Sabra (Layla Beard × mariae)
Red, primrose striped; lip in same color.
Phal. Schöne von Celle (Alice Gloria × Elinor Schaffer)
Phal. Schöne von Unna (Schöne von Celle × Vallehigh)
Pure white to white with yellow green on edges of lip; brown red markings.
Phal. Spitzberg (Opaline × Antarctica)
White with primrose red center.
Phal. Stern von Paradiese (gigantea × Krümline)
Primrose yellow with red dots; lip in the same color.
Phal. Sternthaler (Cafida × fascia)
Yellow with primrose red markings.
Phal. Tiffany (Rosalind × Zauberrose)
Red with strongly colored lip.
Phal. Windspiel (Barbara Mohler × Lady Ruby)
Golden green with carnation red veins and lip.
Phal. Vicadi (Cafida × violacea)
White with red lip and veins.
Phal. Zadian (lueddemanniana × Zada)
White base to sunflower yellow, evenly dotted in red brown.
Phal. Zauberrose (Lippezauber × Zauberrose)
Red with darker lip.

elevations up to 3,300 feet (1,000 m). Blooms from August to November.

Phalaenopsis violacea
Four leaves; leaves are egg-shaped, green; flowers up to 2¼ inches (6 cm) in diameter; greenish white to yellow with carmine red, succes-sive flowerings.
Home: Sumatra and Borneo; as epiphyte near water.
Blooms from June to November.

Crossbreeding Phalaenopsis and Doritis

Doritis pulcherrima is the only species of this genera. It is found from Burma to Sumatra. This orchid is very similar to the epiphyte *Phalaenopsis*, growing at elevations between 300 and 3,900 feet (100 and 1,200 m). It has the same requirements as *Phalaenopsis*. *Doritis* has six to eight leaves that are 4 × 1½ inches (10 × 3.5 cm) in size. The leaves are oblong or lancet shaped; flower stems grow up to 24 inches (60 cm) high. The flowers of *Doritis* are 1 inch (2.5 cm) in diameter. Usually carmine red in color, they can also be pink to white with strong variations.

Doritaenopsis

Doritis × *Phalaenopsis* = *Doritaenopsis (Dpts.)*, 1935.
Dpts. Bryan Wheeler (Phal. Zada × Dpts. Jerry Sue King)
Uniformly purple red.
Dpts. Fuchsia Princess (Dpts. Coral Gleam × D. pulcherrima)
Light carnation red with orange stigma.
Dpts. Herzkönig (Dpts. Michaela × Phal. Coeur As)
Red with red lip and a small white edge.
Dpts. Jaspis (Dpts. Coral Gleam × Phal. Lipperose)
Uniformly purple red.
Dpts. Juela (Dpts. Michaela × Red Judy)
Trailing spike 26 inches (65 cm) long; light purple red with red lip.
Dpts. Mem Clarence Schubert (Phal. Zada × D. pulcherrima)
Purple red with darker lip.
Dpts. Mosel (Dpts. Chauson × Phal. Mad Hatter)
Purple red, with contrasting lip.
Dpts. Parme (Dpts. Red Coral × Phal. Romance)
Uniformly purple red.
Dpts. Ravenswood (Dpts. Mem. Clarence Schubert × Phal. Zada)
Purple red with darker, dotted lip.
Dpts. Stern von Lausanne (Dpts. Rorschach × Phal. mannii)
Purple red with darker center.
Dpts. Youthful (Pueblo Jewel × Phal. Redfan)
Purple red; intensely colored lip with white edge.

Phalaenopsis hybrid

<table>
<tr><td>

Additional Multicolored Hybrids with Phalaenopsis

Phalaenopsis × *Ascocentrum* = *Asconopsis*, 1968

Asconopsis Mini-Coral (Phal. schilleriana × *Ascocentrum miniatum)*

Asconopsis Irene Doktin

Phal. Renanthera = *Renanthopsis*

Renanthopsis Mildred Jameson (Renanthera Monachia × *Phal. stuartiana)*

Sunflower yellow with red dots

Phalaenopsis × *Ascocentrum* × *Vanda* = *Devereuxara*, 1970

1. Dora Ellis (Vandopsis × *Asc. Ophelia) Phalaenopsis* × *Doritis* × *Ascocentrum* = *Beardara*, 1970

1. Bdra. Charles Beard (Dpts. Red Coral × *Asc. miniatum)*

Phal. × *Ascocentrum* × *Renanthera* × *Vanda* = *Stamariara*, 1974

Phal. Ascocentrum × *Doritis* × *Vanda* = *Vandeweghara*, 1975

Phal. Ascocentrum × *Arachnis* × *Vanda* = *Bokchoonara*, 1977

Phal. Ascocentrum × *Rhynchostylis* × *Vanda* = *Himoiara*, 1978

Phal. Ascocentrum × *Vandopsis* = *Richardmitzutaara*, 1978

</td></tr>
</table>

Renanthopsis Mildred Jameson

Paphiopedilum

The so-called Venus Slipper is one of the most loved of all orchids. Part of its attraction is the longevity of its flowers. It belongs to the genus *Paphiopedilum*. This genus consists of about 65 species which range from India to Hong Kong and the Malaysian peninsula and from Indonesia to New Guinea and the Philippines. They are not found in Africa, the Americas, nor in Australia.

Most of these orchids are terres-

Asconopsis Irene Doktin (Phalaenopsis × Ascocentrum)

trial plants. They are typical representatives of the tropical and monsoon forests, where they grow amid the moss and humus on the forest floor. Occasionally, they are found on rocky islands. Some species grow as epiphytes in branch forks. Because of their original environment, they easily adapt to indoor conditions. However, some flourish only in heated greenhouses.

The leaves of *Paphiopedilum* are fleshy, and those that require warmth have marblelike markings. The leaves of those that prefer a cooler, or temperate, climate are almost always green.

The length of the hairy flower stalks varies among different species. The stalks grow out from the center of the leaf clusters. Depending on the species, *Paphiopedilum* orchids have a single flower or several on one stem. The colors are strong and varied. The upper, or dorsal, sepal is usually large and colored in a bright, conspicuous color. This is often called the "flag." The sepals on the opposite side are usually joined behind the lip. Two petals spread stiffly to the side or droop slightly downwards. The third petal has become the lip (labellum). The staminodium is a sterile stamen.

The colors of the flowers range from white to dark mahogany. They are 2 to 5 inches (5 to 12.5 cm) in size. When left on the plant, a flower will often last for six weeks.

Conditions necessary for cultivation

Based on the shape of their leaves, *Paphiopedilum* orchids are divided into three groups:

55

1. Spotted, mottled leaves: These need a minimum temperature of 59°F (15°C). Daytime temperatures may vary between 68 and 77°F (20 and 25°C). The growing cycle does not depend on a specific season.
2. Green leaves: During the winter months and in the spring, nighttime temperatures must be between 50 and 59°F (10 and 15°C). Such temperatures initiate and support vigorous flowering.
3. Leatherlike leaves: These need a dry period of several months and can tolerate temperatures up to 95°F (35°C).

For a short period of time, all three categories will tolerate temperatures as low as 41°F (5°C). However, at lower temperatures, the plants will freeze. The relative humidity should be as constant as possible. During the day, it should be 40 to 70 percent; during the night about 50 to 80 percent is best.

Paphiopedilum belong to the group of orchids that have less need for bright light than other groups. From spring through fall, they need about 6,000 to 7,000 lux; During the winter, 8,000 to 10,000 lux is best. Exposure to direct morning sunlight is to be avoided. The plants need about 14 hours of daylight. Since they cannot store water, they must be kept moist throughout the year. Two growing

Paphiopedilum insigne

phases have to be taken into consideration. When new growth has matured, the root bulbs should only be kept moderately moist. During the active growth cycle, sufficient moisture must be available in case temperatures are on the high side. Depending on the amount of sunlight, the plants should be watered every three to five days. In cloudy weather, once a week is sufficient. In any case, it is advisable to carefully check the degree of moisture in the substrate.

During the active growing cycle, the plants need a high nitrogen fertilizer (about 0.1 to 0.3 percent solution) every two weeks. When flowers begin to appear, the fertilizer (used once a week) should be higher in phosphorus and potash.

Recommended Paphiopedilum Orchids

Species with spotted or mottled leaves

Nighttime temperatures of 64 to 68°F (18 to 20°C), relative humidity 80 percent, and half shade.

Paphiopedilum acmodontum
Whitish green to pink flowers with dark carmine red veins; lip is olive brown.
Home: The Philippines.
Blooms from March to June.

Paphiopedilum argus
Flower has white base; flag has green stripes; petals are black speckled, ends are purple; lip is brown green to purple.
Home: The Philippines, on lime-

Paphiopedilum argus

stone; at elevations of 2,500 to 5,900 feet (750 to 1,800 m).
Blooms from March to June.

Paphiopedilum callosum
Light green leaves with dark green spots; flowers range from green to white and purple to brown and sit on high stems; a large, widely distributed species.
Home: From Thailand to Indochina; at elevations between 1,000 and 3,000 feet (300 and 1,000 m).
Blooms from March to July.

Paphiopedilum hookerae

57

Paphiopedilum hennisianum
Flower has a whitish green flag with brown veins; petals are white and green with purple middle stripes; lip is olive brown.
Home: The Philippines.
Blooms from February to June.

Paphiopedilum hookerae
Flower is cream greenish color with purple veins; petals are green with black speckles, ends are purple as is the lip.
Home: Borneo.
Blooms from April to June.

Paphiopedilum mastersianum
Flower has green flag with white edges; petals and lip are copper colored with black markings.
Home: The island of Ambon.
Blooms from April till July.

Paphiopedilum sukhakulii
Flowers are whitish green with brown mahogany colored lip.
Home: Northern Thailand.
Blooms from March to July.

Paphiopedilum tonsum
Green yellow flower with purple.
Home: Sumatra at elevations of 3,300 feet (1,000 m).
Blooms from February to July.

Paphiopedilum urbanianum
Flag is white green; petals and lip are brown to purple in color.
Home: The Philippines.
Blooms from February to July.

Species with speckled, thicker leaves
Nighttime temperatures about 68°F (20°C); relative humidity 80 percent; half shade.

Paphiopedilum bellatulum
Broad leaves; white, purple-speckled flower has a short stem.
Home: Burma and northern Thailand, at elevations between 1,300 and 3,300 feet (400 and 1,000 m); grows on lime or loamy soil.
Blooms from April till August.

Paphiopedilum delenatii
Small plant with light green speckled leaves; flower is white, rose, and red; needs a warm climate.
Home: Indochina.
Blooms from March till June.

Paphiopedilum niveum
Leaves are light green with dark green, marblelike markings, underside is red brown; flower is white with red dots; loves high temperatures.
Home: Malaysia and Indochina.
Blooms from July to November.

Paphiopedilum niveum

Paphiopedilum villosum

Species with thin, green leaves
Nighttime temperatures around 54°F (12°C); partial shade.

Paphiopedilum fairieanum
Flower is white with carmine red veins and hairs.
Home: Himalayan mountains, at elevations of 4,000 to 6,500 feet (1,200 to 2,200 m); near water on steep banks in humus and lime soil.
Blooms from October till December.

Paphiopedilum hirsutissimum
Flower has green grey speckled flag; petals are yellow green to brown and wavy; lip is green brown.
Home: From northern India to Thailand; at elevations of 3,300 to 6,000 feet (1,000 to 1,800 m) in lime soil.
Blooms from February till June.

Paphiopedilum insigne
Flower is yellow green with white and brown spots; lip is amber colored and has many different shapes.
Home: Himalayas, at elevations of 3,900 to 6,600 feet (1,200 to

2,000 m); grows on moss in lime soil.
Blooms from November till January.

Paphiopedilum villosum
Yellow green flower has brown markings; lip is yellow brown.
var. boxallii: Flag is densely speckled with black purple.
Home: Assam, Burma, and Vietnam, at elevations of about 3,300 to 5,200 feet (1,000 to 1,600 m).
Blooms from November till February.

Species with thick, green leaves
Nighttime temperatures around 60°F (16°C); partial shade to sunny.

Paphiopedilum parishii
Flower is white green to brown to purple; petals droop; produces several flowers; must be kept moist.
Home: Himalayas, Thailand, southern China; grows on trees and tree ferns.
Blooms from April to September.

Paphiopedilum parishii

Species with leatherlike leaves

Nighttime temperatures around 68°F (20°C), relative humidity 80 percent; light, sunny location.

Paphiopedilum philippinense
Four to six flowers; flowers are cream colored with red brown stripes; petals are long, drooping, and twisted; lip is yellow.
Home: The Philippines, at elevations of 3,300 to 6,600 feet (1,000 to 2,000 m) and on the coasts.
Blooms from June till August.

Paphiopedilum praestans
Produces several flowers similar to those mentioned above.
Home: New Guinea; grows in soil rich in lime.
Blooms from June to August.

Paphiopedilum philippinense

Paphiopedilum hybrids

Paphiopedilum hybrids come in all possible shades and colors, from white to yellow and green to deep red and brown, in solid colors, speckled, or striped. The size of the flowers also varies, but most of them are long-lasting.

In the last few years, the interest in primary hybrids has vastly increased. These are produced by

---

White Green Striped Paphiopedilum Hybrids

P. Goultenianum (curtisii × callosum)
P. Holdenii (callosum × Maudiae)
P. Maudiae (callosum × lawrenceanum)
P. Onyx Alba (Goultenianum album × Maudiae)
P. Rosetti (insigne × Maudiae)

New Bellatulum Hybrids

P. Charles Richman (bellatulum × barbatum)
P. Charles Sladden (bellatulum × glaucophyllum)
P. Demura (bellatulum × Blendia)
P. Evelyn Röllke (bellatulum × sukhakulii)
P. Iona (bellatulum × fairieanum)
P. Lawrebel (bellatulum × lawrenceanum)
P. Olenus (bellatulum × ciliolare)
P. Paris (bellatulum × stonei)

Fairieanum Hybrids

P. Chapmanii (fairieanum × curtisii)
P. Diane (fairieanum × chamberlainianum)
P. Faire-Maud (fairieanum × Maudiae)
P. John Clark (fairieanum × Harrisianum)
P. Juno (fairieanum × collosum)
P. Miss D. S. Brown (fairieanum × Gowernianum)
P. Sibyl (fairieanum × Goultenianum)

Paphiopedilum Dellaina (delenatii × chamberlainianum)

Paphiopedilum hybrid (primulinum × delenatii)

crossbreeding two original speci-mens; the hybrids usually grow more vigorously than their parents and show very interesting color combinations.

Some P. Delenatii Hybrids (mostly pink)
P. Alix (delenatii × Calvi)
P. appletonianum × P. delenatii
P. Darling (lawrenceanum × Madame Martinet)
P. Dellaina (delenatii × chamber-lainianum)
P. Delophyllum (delenatii × glauco-phyllum)
P. Delrosi (delenatii × rothschildianum)
P. Deporte (delenatii × primulinum)
P. Madame Martinet (delenatii × callosum)
P. Mercedes Gallup (delenatii × Vanda M. Pearman)
P. Neerach (delenatii × gardineri)
P. Vanda M. Pearman (delenatii × bellatulum)

Paphiopedilum That Produce Multiple Flowers	
P. A. de Lairesse (rothschildianum × curtisii)	*P. Transvaal (r. × chamberlainianum)*
P. Andronicus (r. × victoria-mariae)	*P. Vacuna (r. × villosum)*
P. Elie de Rothschild (r. × San Actaeus)	*P. Vanguard (r. × glaucophyllum)*
P. Excelsior (r. × Harrisianum)	*P. Wiertzianum (r. × lawrenceanum)*
P. Houghtoniae (r. × haynaldianum)	*P. W.R. Lee (r. × superbiens)*
P. Janta Stage (r. × sukhakulii)	*P. Constance (stonei × curtisii)*
P. l'Ansonii (r. × Morganiae)	*P. Imperial Jade (stonei × primulinum)*
P. Lady Isabel (r. × stonei)	*P. Mount Toro (stonei × philippinense)*
P. Oakes Ames (r. × ciliolare)	*P. Stone Ground (stonei × glauco-phyllum)*
P. Rolfei (r. × bellatulum)	*P. stonei × P. insigne*
P. Roth-Maud (r. × Maudiae)	*P. Bufordiense (philippinense × argus)*
P. Saint Swithin (r. × philippinense)	*P. Helvetia (philippinense × chamber-lainianum)*
P. Shillianum (r. × Gowernianum)	*P. Recovery (philippinense × sukhakulii)*
P. Solon (r. × tonsum)	

Paphiopedilum hybrids

Additional Primary Paphiopedilum Hybrids

P. A. W. Sutton (chamberlainianum × niveum)

P. Bengal Lancers (parishii × haynaldianum)

P. Canari (primulinum × Dorasire)

P. Charles Steinmetz (lawrenceanum × roebbelinii)

P. Colbert (curtisii × Alain Gerbault)

P. Colorkuli (concolor × sukhakulii)

P. Cymatodes (curtisii × superbiens)

P. Dusty Miller (F. C. Puddle × Chardmore)

P. Gigi (Sheba × Momag)

P. Glowyn (Cuhur × Paeony)

P. Grand Combin (Ernst Gunzenhauser × Fred Cosanka)

P. Joggae (praestans × glaucophyllum)

P. Lippesonne

P. Makuli (sukhakulii × Maudiae)

P. Miller's Daughter (Chantal × Dusty Miller)

P. Recoutre (curtisii × Procustes)

P. Rosewood (Paeony × Gitana)

P. Sophomore (lawrenceanum × Chardmore)

P. Utgard (chamberlainianum × glaucophyllum)

P. Vercingetorix (curtisii × Shillianum)

P. Véronique (Hortense × Shillianum)

Paphiopedilum Dusty Miller

Cattleya

The 60 natural species of the genus *Cattleya* range from Central and South America to the Caribbean. Individual species grow as epiphytes or lithophytes at different elevations. *Cattleya* usually have cylindrical pseudobulbs or rhizomes that carry one or more leaves. Based on the number of leaves, one can distinguish between two groups: the species with one leaf usually has only three flowers, which are normally quite large. The species with two leaves usually has several flowers (up to 20).

The flower stem appears at the tip of the rhizome between the leaves at their base. The growth is sympodial; the plant produces a new shoot at the base of each pseudobulb every year.

In addition to species hybrids, the result of crossbreeding some 20 species, there are also genera hybrids. This is the reason why *Cattleya* bloom throughout the year. The prime time for flowering is during the winter months and in the spring. The colors of the flowers range from pure white to dark lavender. *Cattleya* can also be successfully crossed with close relatives, resulting in a large variety of shapes and brilliant colors.

Important genus hybrids are:
Brassavola × *Cattleya* = *Brassocattleya (Bc.)*
Brassavola × *Laelia* × *Cattleya* = *Brassolaeliocattleya (Blc.)*

Cattleya loddigesii

63

Laeliocattleya hybrid

Laelia × Cattleya = Laeliocattleya (Lc.)
Brassavola × Laelia × Sophronitis × Cattleya = Potinara (Pot.)
Sophronitis × Cattleya = Sophrocattleya (Sc.)
Sophronitis × Laelia × Cattleya = Sophrolaeliocattleya (Slc.)

Conditions for cultivation

During the summer, temperatures should be between 64 and 75°F (18 and 24°C). With high humidity (70 to 80 percent) and with constant air movement, *Cattleya* are able to tolerate higher temperatures. Nighttime temperatures during the summer should be 54 to 61°F (12 to 16°C).

During the winter, daytime temperatures should be at least 54°F (12°C) and nighttime temperatures should not fall below 50°F (10°C). Humidity should be at least 50 percent. With higher temperatures, it is necessary to provide a humidity of 70 percent. The humidity can be lower during the night. Humidity can be increased by using a container lined with gravel.

Cattleya and its relatives can tolerate much light. In the case of a hardened plant, even full sun is possible. In general, 20,000 to 30,000 lux are sufficient.

During times of intense sun, some shade should be provided. This is especially the case during late

Laeliocattleya, red flower

winter and at the beginning of spring, since the plants are not used to bright light. Also, during the summer, the plants should be shaded during the middle of the day; morning light, however, is very important. At the end of August, shading can be discontinued.

Plants in bloom and very young plants need to be shaded from bright sunlight, particularly after they have been repotted. Good air circulation lowers the surface temperature of the leaves, dries them, and reduces the danger of fungal and viral infections.

During active growth, the soil must be moist and airy. The plants need to be thoroughly watered, but root bulbs should be allowed to dry out between waterings. During the summer, leaves can be sprayed or misted in the morning.

Cattleya

65

During the summer, these plants must be watered at least once a week; when temperatures are high, water two or three times a week. From October on, watering every two to three weeks is sufficient, but spraying should be increased.

The ideal temperature of the water for watering is about 64°F (18°C). A pH value of 5.5 to 6 is best.

Once a month during the summer, the substrate should be thoroughly washed out with distilled water and fertilized.

When new shoots appear, the plant needs to be fed with every watering using 0.08 to 0.1 percent NPK (nitrogen, phosphorus, potassium) 15:10:12 fertilizer; during active growth, use 0.08 to 0.1 percent NPK 10:10:10. No feeding is required during the winter. When flowering begins, fertilize with 0.25 to 0.4 percent NPK 10:10:12 with every watering. With bark substrates, the same concentration of NPK 30:10:10 is recommended. Weekly watering is necessary during active growth.

Cattleya can be divided into three or four parts. Shoot development is supported by spraying with a sodium solution available in specialty nurseries. Experience has shown that *Cattleya* does well in a substrate consisting of coarse pine bark, fern roots, charcoal, and peat moss in a 2:2:2:1 mixture.

Influence of temperature and daylight on Cattleya

Cattleya and its hybrids can be di-

Cattleya forbesii

vided in two groups according to the flowering period.

1. Day-neutral plants usually have two leaves (bifoliate) for each rhizome. Examples are: *C. amethystoglossa, C. aurantiaca, C. bicolor, C. bowringiana, C. dowiana, C. forbesii, C. granulosa, C. guttata, C. intermedia, C. loddigesii* (syn. *C.*

Cattleya trianae

66

harrisoniae), C. skinneri.

These plants are at rest from October to the middle of February. The plants prepare for flowering with high light intensity and day and night temperature differences of 15°F (8°C) during the summer.

2. Other plants need short days and usually have only one leaf per rhyzome (unifoliate). These require low temperatures of about 55°F (13°C) during the short days from the middle of October to the middle of April in order to prepare for flowering. The development of flowers starts between December and February. The following orchids belong to this group: *C. labiata, C. mossiae, C. percivaliana, C. trianae,* and *C. schroederae.*

Bifoliate original orchids
Cattleya aclandiae
An epiphyte; basic color is carmine red; one to two flowers; many variations.

Cattleya aurantiaca

Home: Brazil (Bahia).
Blooms from June to September.

Cattleya aurantiaca
Flowers are relatively small and orange red.
Home: Central America; epiphyte and lithophyte at elevations of 2,300 to 4,900 feet (700 to 1,500 m).
Blooms from April to June.

Cattleya loddigesii
Produces several flowers, pink, white, and yellow in color.
Home: Southern Brazil (mountainous regions).
Blooms from July till October.

Cattleya schilleriana
Scented flowers, brown green; lip is light carmine red with darker veins.
Home: Brazil.
Blooms from July to October.

Cattleya skinneri
Produces several flowers, light violet red.
Home: Central America; an epiphyte at elevations up to 4,000 feet (1,200 m); therefore, has no rest period.
Blooms from March till November.

Unifoliate original orchids
Cattleya dowiana
Large, scented, light yellow flowers; lip is cone shaped and velvety purple in color with gold yellow veins in the center.
Home: Costa Rica (in rain forests);

67

Cattleya dowiana

an epiphyte at elevations from 650 to 3,300 feet (200 to 1,000 m); therefore, cultivate in warm and humid climates; during rest periods, temperature should be 64°F (18°C). Blooms from August to October.

Cattleya Hybrids

For a long time, these orchids were favorites of orchid lovers because of the size of the flowers and the scent. Today, although *Phalaenopsis* has taken over the "number one" position, very interesting crossbreeding of *Cattleya* has taken place.

C. Guatemalensis (skinneri × labiata)
Very easy care; blooms in the spring.

C. Iran Imperial Coronation
Dark carmine red; blooms in the summer.

C. Iris (bicolor × dowiana "Aurea")
Blooms in the summer and fall.

C. Money Maker
Multi-flowering, large flowers; blooms in the spring.

C. Odalisque
White flowers; blooms in the spring.

C. Portia coerulea (bowringiana × labiata)
Blooms in the fall and winter.

C. Schwanendaunen
White, multi-flowering; blooms in the summer.

Cattleya hybrid (bowringiana × labiata)

Laelia and Its Relatives

Laelia, Epidendrum, Brassavola (syn. *Rhyncholaelia*), *Sophronitis* and *Schomburgkia* are all relatives of the *Cattleya* orchid. *Laelia* is most closely related to *Cattleya* in form. There are about 35 different species, ranging from Mexico to Brazil. These orchids grow as epiphytes. The flowers are very long-lasting.

Conditions for cultivation

These plants require nighttime temperatures of about 55 to 61°F (13 to 16°C) and daytime temperatures of about 64 to 75°F (18 to 24°C). They also profit from four to eight hours of direct sunlight. The relative humidity should be about 50 to 80 percent.

Flower development can be supported by providing sufficient air movement and a decrease in watering and spraying at the end of the growth period.

The substrate should be a mixture of bark, *Osmunda* fibre, and orchid chips. The potting mixture should only be watered when it is completely dry. Feed the orchid every third watering with a fertilizer obtained from a specialty nursery or shop. Do not feed during the rest period. The substrate should be kept somewhat cooler and moister at that time.

Hybrids with thick leaves need a rest period. During this period, the plant needs more light. Propagation is the same as for *Cattleya*.

Laelia harpophylla
Fleshy, vermilion to salmon colored flowers.
Home: Brazil.
Blooms in the winter and spring.

Laelia purpurata
Has white to light carmine and purple colored flowers; lip markings vary widely.

Laelia harpophylla

Laelia purpurata

Home: Brazil; grows as an epiphyte and lithophyte near the coast; in sandy soil, grows as a terrestrial plant.
Blooms in the spring.

Laelia hybrids
Hybrids produced from *Laelia* and its relatives have interested orchid lovers because of the hybrids' colors, long-lasting flowers, the abundance of flowers they produce, as well as the long stems of the floral axes.

Laeliocattleya Alma Wichmann (Golden Joy × Edgar van Belle)
Flower is primrose yellow with light red dots; lip is orange yellow.
Blooms in the spring and summer.

Lc. Belle O'Bronze (bicolor × Edgar van Belle)
Blooms in the fall and winter.

Lc. Flämmchen (C. Iris × cinnabarina)
Flower is yellow orange to red.
Blooms in the spring.

Lc. Harold Carlson (Irvin Dietsche × E. Enid)
Blooms in the spring, summer, and winter.

Lc. Max and Moritz (Elinor × Louise Geogoriana)
Long-lasting, orange colored flowers.
Blooms in the winter.

Lc. Wintermärchen
Pink flowers.
Blooms in the winter.

70

Epidendrum and Its Close Relatives

Originally, there were nearly 1,000 species of *Epidendrum* orchids. However, the botanical classification has been overhauled in the last decades. Since the differences for the orchid lover are not that apparent, many species are still offered under their old names.

Epidendrum is represented in the whole of the tropical and subtropical American regions from Florida to Bolivia and Paraguay. These orchids grow as epiphytes, lithophytes, and as terrestrial plants.

The members of this group display many different shapes. The differences go from unifoliate species with a few shoots, to those that are bifoliate with densely arranged leaves. The floral axis is always at the end of the stem. Flower petals can be very similar, but also very different. The column is fused with the lip.

Epidendrum ciliare

Sectional, spindle-shaped shoots, one to two leaves; new shoots secrete a sticky substance; flowers are scented and yellow green; lip is three-lobed and white and yellow. Home: Mexico, Brazil, and Peru, at elevations of 2,600 to 4,900 feet (800 to 1,500 m); grows as an epiphyte and lithophyte.
Blooms in the winter (as well as in late summer).

Epidendrum radicans

Large shoots, up to 7 feet (2 m) in height; bifoliate, leaves longish to egg-shaped; orange red flowers are

Epidendrum radicans

71

A Few Epidendrum Hybrids

Epicattleya Matutine (C. bowringiana × Epid. ibaguense)

Epicattleya Tell (Epi. vitellinum × C. labiata)

In general, all have good growth and flowering characteristics.

Epilaelia Hardyana (Epi. ciliare × Laelia anceps)

Medium-sized plant with flowers that are similar to *Cattleya*; likes well-lit location; an interesting plant for the beginner.

Epilaeliocattleya Kahili (Lc. Kahili Kea × Epid. mariae)

Medium-sized flower similar to *Cattleya*, varied colors, long-lasting; likes location with plenty of light; keep moist during active growing period.

---

cymose, at the end of the stalk, long-lasting; lip is three-lobed and split. Home: Mexico and Guatemala. Blooms throughout the year (mainly during the winter).

Encyclia

This genus includes about 130 species. It is found from Florida to southern Brazil. The species have a rather similar appearance: The pseudobulbs grow tightly together, and there are one to three leathery leaves at the end of the stem (as is the case with the floral axis). An important characteristic is that the lip is not joined to the column.

This is a light-loving plant; however, it does not like direct sunlight. It should have good air circulation. The plant prefers to be moist and fed during active growth. During the summer, daytime temperatures should be around 68 to 77°F (20 to 25°C); during the night, 63 to 68°F (17 to 20°C). During the rest period, the ideal temperature is 59°F (15°C). Development of flowering is supported by reducing the amount of watering, spraying at the end of the growth period, and assuring sufficient air circulation.

Encyclia mariae
(syn. *Epidendrum mariae*; syn. *Hormidium mariae*)
Yellow green, white flowers.
Home: Mexico; grows as an epiphyte at elevations of 5,300 to 7,200 feet (1,600 to 2,200 m).
Blooms in the summer.

Encyclia vitellina
(syn. *Epidendrum vitellinum*; syn. *Hormidium vitellinum*)
Leaves are blue green and frosted; flowers are salmon red to yellow orange.
Home: Mexico and Guatemala, at elevations of 4,900 to 8,500 feet (1,500 to 2,600 m).
Blooms in the summer and fall.

Brassavola

This genus has about 15 species and is found in the tropical regions of the Americas, including Argentina. The

Encyclia vitellina

plants grow as epiphytes on cacti or rocks at elevations up to 2,000 feet (600 m). The pseudobulbs are stem-like in shape and carry one (and occasionally two) tubular, succulent leaves. Flowers develop on the edge of the leaves. The flowers consist of almost uniformly shaped yelow green petals, often with a large, white lip.

Daytime temperatures should be around 64 to 75°F (18 to 24°C) and 55 to 61°F (13 to 16°C) during the night. Plants from this genus need a relatively large amount of light. During active growth, the plants should be provided with artificial light (approximately 10,000 lux) for an additional three to five hours.

Relative humidity in the summer is best around 40 to 70 percent; and in the winter, about 40 to 60 percent.

Brassavola cucullata
Single, scented flowers.
Blooms in the summer months and in the fall in tropical forests.

Brassavola nodosa
Home: Central America, at elevations up to 1,600 feet (500 m); grows as epiphyte on cacti and mangrove trees with a dry period during times of heavy dew.
Blooms from summer to winter.

There are not many crossbreeds involving *Brassavola*. Most of these result from *Rhyncholaelia digbyana*, which is registered under the name *Brassavola*. Here are the identifying characteristics of *Rhyncholaelia*:

73

Brassavola nodosa

Rhyncholaelia digbyana
This species originally belonged to the *Brassavola* family. These orchids can be found in regions from southern Mexico to Honduras. They grow in rain forests at elevations up to 4,900 feet (1,500 m). The pseudobulbs are 6 inches (15 cm) long, flat, and tubular at the base. They have a frosted, narrow, elliptical leaf.

Flowers are large and greenish white; the lip is large, fringed at the edges, and greenish.
Blooms from spring to fall.

Rhyncholaelia glauca
This orchid is small. It grows as an epiphyte on wood. During the active growing period, and after the

---

Important Hybrids
Brassiolaeliocattleya (Blc.) Allergarten
Flowers are lilac pink with a darker lip.
Blooms during the summer.
Blc. Ergolz (C. bicolor × Blc. Malvern)
Blc. Hilda (Blc. Sindorax × C. Queen Mary)
Blooms in the winter and spring.
Blc. Malworth (Lc. Charlesworthii × Blc. Malvern)
Blc. Superstar (Blc. Simoun × Lc. Canberra)
Blc. Wichmanns Liebling
Flowers are light carmine red with a darker, fringed lip and yellow speckles.
Blooms in the summer.

flowers have wilted, the plant requires a great deal of light, but little moisture for the roots. When the roots are growing, the plant must be watered and fertilized. Repotting should be done very infrequently; the proper time for repotting would be the beginning of the growing period.

Blooms from late winter to spring.

Schomburgkia

This genus has 15 species and is found in regions ranging from Mexico to Brazil. Growth is similar to that of the *Cattleya*. These orchids, growing as epiphytes, love a bright, sunny location. Flower stems are usually long, and the plant is multi-flowered. Daytime temperatures should be 64 to 75°F (18 to 24°C), and at night about 55 to 61°F (13 to 16°C).

Schomburgkia tibicinis
Fleshy, scented flowers, 3¼ inches (8 cm) in diameter, red brown violet, partially veined, on long stems.
Home: Mexico and Guatemala.
Blooms in the spring and summer.
Tip: Care is similar to that of *Cattleya*. The plants require bright loca-

Schomburgkia tibicinis

tions with temperatures up to 86°F (30°C), and at night around 43 to 46°F (6 to 8°C).

Sophronitis

This dwarf orchid has large flowers. It is found on the east coast of Brazil at elevations between 2,300 and 3,300 feet (700 and 1,000 m), growing as an epiphyte on trees. There are seven species.

The pseudobulbs are round or flattened. Each produces one egg-shaped, leathery leaf.

Sophronitis coccinea
Flowers are up to 3¼ inches (8 cm) in diameter, salmon red and yellow with great variability.
Blooms in the winter and spring.

Important Hybrids

Schombocattleya = (Schomburgkia × Cattleya)
Dillonara (Dill.) = (Schomburgkia × Epidendrum × Laelia)
Northenera (North.) = (Schomburgkia × Cattleya × Epidendrum × Laelia)
Westara (West.) = (Schomburgkia × Brassavola × Broughtonia × Cattleya × Laelia)

Sophronitis coccinea

Sophronitis—Hybrids

These usually have brilliantly colored flowers.

Sophrolaeliocattleya (Sc.) (Sophronitis × Laelia × Cattleya)

Slc. Jewel Box "Sherzerade." Frequently propagated species with light red, large flowers. Blooms in the spring.

Slc. Lippstadt (Lc. Belle of Celle × Slc. Anzac) Carnation to primrose red with blue violet lip.

Potinara = (Sophronitis × Brassavola × Cattleya × Laelia)

Izumiara = (Sophronitis × Cattleya × Epidendrum × Laelia × Schomburgkia)

Odontoglossum and Rossioglossum

Since the 1980s, some of the species formerly considered to be *Odontoglossum* are now separately identified under the new name, *Rossioglossum. Odontoglossum* are found all over Central and South America. About 100 species prefer elevations of 4,900 to 9,900 feet (1,500 to 3,000 m). All *Odontoglossum* species have egg-shaped pseudobulbs with flattened sides. Fringed sepals and petals are typical. This species has large yellowish brown flowers and grows as epiphytes.

Odontoglossum rossii

Conditions for cultivation

The species and hybrids are divided into three groups:

1. Those requiring cool conditions: *O. crispum, O. pulchellum, O. rossii, O. cordatum*

   Temperatures: Winter—daytime 54°F (12°C), nighttime 50°F (10°C); summer—daytime up to 59°F (15°C), nighttime 54 to 59°F (12 to 15°C).

   Rest period: November till middle or end of March. Relative humidity should be 50 to 60 percent, and the soil surface should be kept dry. Relative humidity during the summer should be 80 to 90 percent.

2. Those requiring cool to temperate conditions: *O. bictoniense, O. pendulum, O. uroskinneri.*

   Temperatures: Winter—daytime 59°F (15°C), nighttime 50°F (10°C); summer—daytime 68 to 77°F (20 to 25°C), not to exceed 82°F (28°C), nighttime 59°F (15°C). Humidity as above.

   Rest period: Middle of October till the end of March.

3. Those requiring temperate conditions: *O. krameri,* without a rest period.

   Temperatures: Winter—daytime 59°F (15°C), nighttime 54°F (12°C); summer—daytime 68 to 77°F (20 to 25°C), nighttime 61°F (16°C).

   Relative humidity should be adjusted according to the temperature.

Flower development is encouraged when the plant is given a lot of light (50,000 lux) and increased assimilation. These are combined with a dry period that should start when the bulbs begin to mature and

Odontoglossum Species

continue until the flower stems begin to appear.

During the winter, the plants can tolerate direct sunlight. When outside during the summer, it is best to keep them shaded under a tree. Frequent rainfall is tolerated when the substrate is sufficiently porous. Since these orchids grow in montane forests, a constant, high relative humidity is recommended. Don't forget to spray. During the winter it is important to provide sufficient fresh air.

The plant needs to be kept evenly moist from the beginning to the end of the growing period. The best pH value is around 4.5.

Odontoglossum bictoniense
Flowers are yellow green with pink markings; lip is heart-shaped and pink in color.
Home: Mexico to El Salvador; generally epiphytic at elevations from 5,300 to 10,500 feet (1,600 to 3,200 m).
Blooms from October to April.

Odontoglossum cordatum
Flowers are star-shaped, yellow with dark brown speckles and edges; lip is white with somewhat brown speckles.
Home: Mexico to Colombia and Venezuela; grows as epiphytes in damp montane forests at elevations

Rossioglossum grande

of 6,600 to 9,900 feet (2,000 to 3,000 m).
Blooms from July till August.

Odontoglossum crispum
Flowers are white with a red tinge and red brown speckles.
Home: Colombia and Peru, at elevations up to 10,500 feet (3,200 m).
Blooms from February till June.

Odontoglossum rossii
Flowers have a white base with red brown speckles; lip is wavy with a few brown speckles.
Home: Mexico to Nicaragua; grows as an epiphyte at elevations of 9,900 feet (3,000 m).
Blooms from January till May.

Rossioglossum (Odontoglossum) grande
Flowers up to 4¾ inches (12 cm) in diameter, yellow base with chestnut brown edges; lip is three-lobed with white, red brown, and yellow speckles.
Home: Mexico and Guatemala, at elevations of 8,900 feet (2,700 m).
Blooms from September to December.

Odontoglossum hybrids
Crossbreeding with primary hybrids has occurred since 1904 with *Odm. crispum*, *Odm. harryanum*, *Odm. nobile*, *Odm. rossii*, and *Odm. triumphans*. The goal has been to produce good flowering species.

Today, the most important hybrids are *Odm. Pescalo* 1953, *Odm. Stropheon* 1957, and *Odm. Yukon Harbor* 1959. Around 1960, breeding took a new direction. Other genera

provided more brilliant colors and needed less complicated conditions for cultivation.

The following are some of these new hybrids: *Odm. Anneliese Rothenberger* (bictoniense × Goldrausch), *Odm. Bicross* (bictoniense × rossii), *Odm. Burkhard Holm* (Anneliese Rothenberger × Goldrausch), *Odm. Cristor* (crispum × Tordonia), *Odm. Hambühren*, *Odm. Hans Koch*.

Oncidium

Because of their shape, the 700 species of this genus are called "Butterfly Orchids." They can be found in the tropical regions of Florida, the West Indies, and Mexico, all the way to southern Brazil. This broad range is the reason that so many different cultivating conditions have to be observed. *Oncidium* orchids are sympodial and bloom all year long. The shape of the plants is similar to *Odontoglossum* and the *Miltonia*. Some *Oncidium* have flat pseudobulbs; others have round, onionlike leaves; and still others have leaves similar to those of the iris. The flower stems are upright. Some have only one or two blossoms; others have hundreds. The flowers themselves have basic markings that vary only in shape, size, and color.

Conditions necessary for cultivation
Oncidium adapt to different climates more easily than *Odontoglossum* and *Miltonia* orchids. Most can be kept in conditions similar to those men-

79

tioned for *Cattleya* orchids. The only exceptions are those with large flowers. Nighttime temperatures of 59°F (15°C) and daytime temperature of 70°F (21°C) are best (higher when exposed to the sun). Those with tough leaves and without pseudobulbs can tolerate even higher temperatures. Relative humidity should be about 50 percent.

The best light is 20,000 to 40,000 lux; tough-leaved species can tolerate full sun (which is 80,000 lux); plants in bloom should be shaded. Air circulation is particularly important when temperatures are high. Plants in bloom should be watered sufficiently—more frequently than is recommended for *Cattleya* orchids.

Oncidium crispum
Flowers are red brown; lip is golden yellow in the center with many variations.
Home: Brazil.
Blooms from August to December.

Oncidium pulchellum
Has no pseudobulbs; color of the small flowers ranges from white to pink; lip has yellow speckles.
Home: Jamaica.
Blooms from June to August.

Oncidium splendidum
Leathery, V-shaped leaves on flat pseudobulb; floral axes up to 3 feet (1 m) long; flowers are yellow green

Oncidium varicosum

Odontocidium (Odm. uro-skinneri × Onc. anderanum)

with red brown speckles; lip is lemon yellow.
Home: Guatemala.
Blooms from December to February.
Tip: Rest period begins before shoots have finished growing.

Oncidium triquetrum
Similar to *Oncidium pulchellum*; basic flower color is white green with purple speckles; lip is white with purple speckles and stripes and orange yellow specks.
Home: Jamaica.
Blooms from August to October.

Oncidium varicosum
Yellow, loosely branched flowers; lip has characteristic shape; petals are striped in yellow, red, and brown.
Home: Brazil.
Blooms from September to February.

Miltonia and Miltoniopsis

The 25 different species are found from Costa Rica to Paraguay. The pseudobulbs are egg-shaped and surrounded by low-growing leaves. Flowers develop from the axis of the

---

Oncidium Hybrids
Only produced since 1957.
Onc. Catherine Wilson (Onc. triquetrum × Onc. pulchellum)
Onc. Red Belt (Onc. Golden Glow × Onc. triquetrum)
Onc. Golden Cascade (Onc. Varimyre × Onc. varicosum)
Onc. Golden Sunset (Onc. Stanley Smith × Onc. Tiny Tim)
Onc. Goldrausch (Onc. forbesii × Onc. Varimyre)
Onc. Tiny Tim (Onc. triquetrum × Onc. intermedium)
Odontocidium = (Odontoglossum × Oncidium)
Odcdm. Autumn Glow (Odm. bictoniense × Onc. olivaceum)
Odcdm. Autumn Tints (Odm. bictoniense × Onc. forbesii)
Odcdm. Tiger Hambühren (Onc. tigrinum × Odm. Goldrausch)
Odcdm. Vera Stolze (Onc. sarcodes × Odm. bictoniense)

uppermost leaves. The petals look very much alike, and the lip is large and shows no division.

Conditions for cultivation

Miltonia orchids are epiphytes, but since they have only very small pseudobulbs and soft leaves, they need attentive care.

Climate conditions are very similar to those required for *Cattleya*—particularly the Brazilian species. However in contrast to *Cattleya* orchids, these like more shade. Those from Colombia prefer a cool, airy, and shaded location in the summer. During the winter, they like a somewhat warm to temperate climate of about 64 to 68°F (18 to 20°C). Nighttime temperatures can fall as low as 54 to 59°F (12 to 15°C), which sup-

ports good growth. Relative humidity should be at least 60 percent; 80 percent is even better. High humidity during the night is very good.

It is especially important to keep the root bulbs of *Miltonia* constantly moist. Feeding the plant every two weeks during active growth assures good development. During the rest period, the plant should only be fed every four weeks. The substrate must be porous.

Miltonia candida
Flowers are orange with dark brown speckles; lip is violet with white.
Home: Brazil.
Blooms from August to October.

Miltonia spectabilis
White to greenish flowers with white to carmine red lip.
Home: Venezuela and Brazil.
Blooms from July to October.

Miltonia Hybrids
These have long-lasting flowers, but they are not very good as cut flowers.
Odontonia (Odtna) = Odontoglossum (Odm.) × Miltonia (Milt.)
These bloom freely and have colorful flowers. They do not tolerate high temperatures.
Miltonidium (Mtdm.) = Miltonia × Oncidium
These have striking flowers in brilliant colors.

Miltonia spectabilis

Cochlioda

Cochlioda are very close relatives of the *Odontoglossum*. They have brilliant colors, pink and red flowers, and dark green leaves growing on top of pseudobulbs that are wider than they are long. Growing requirements are much like those for *Odontoglossum*. However, these need less humidity.

Cochlioda noezliana

Loosely branched flower clusters as long as 20 inches (50 cm); 10 to 15 flowers are orange red with yellow

Odontioda (Cochlioda hybrid)

Cochlioda Hybrids
These are much sought after for their brilliant colors.
Odontioda (Oda) = Odontoglossum × Cochlioda
Oda Feuerkugel, Oda Franz Wichmann, Oda Karl Heinz Hanisch, Oda Lippetor, Oda Lippstadt, Oda Mainaustern
Vuylstekeara (Vuyl.) = Odontoglossum × Cochlioda × Miltonia
Vuyl. Cambria "Plush" Vuyl. Edna Vuyl. Rothaut, Vuyl. Yokara
Wilsonara (Wils.) = Odontoglossum × Cochlioda × Oncidium
Wils. Annemarie Wichmann, Wils. Celle, Wils. Franz Wichmann, Wils. Hambührer
Stern, Wils. Intermezzo

speckles.
Home: Peru.
Blooms from December to April.

Comparettia

This genus includes seven species; they are found from Central America to Brazil. The plants are small and grow as epiphytes with long flower stems. The flowers are usually brilliantly colored. The lip is large and has intensely bright colors.

Conditions for cultivation

During the active growing period, the plant needs daytime temperatures from 64 to 68°F (18 to 20°C) and nighttime temperatures of 50 to 59°F (10 to 15°C). The humidity should be 50 to 70 percent or higher.

This orchid needs a shaded location. The light intensity should not exceed 5,000 lux. During the rest period, the plant needs little water. The best substrate is fine-grained bark and fern roots. If the substrate is kept too dry, it is almost impossible to prevent infections of red spider, thrips, and mites.

Comparettia falcata
Pseudobulbs are 1¼ inches (3 cm)

Comparettia Hybrids

Odontorettia (Odrta) Mandarine =
(Odm. bictoniense × Comp. speciosa)
Brilliant colors from yellow orange to red.
Odontorettia (Odrta) Violetta = (Odm. bictoniense × Comp. falcata)
Flowers are rose primrose red; lip is strongly red in color.

Odontorettia Violetta (hybrid) ⟩

high and have one leaf; flowers are carmine red and shaded in yellow red.
Home: Colombia and Peru.
Blooms from June to September.

Dendrobium and Hybrids

Dendrobium, with over 1,000 species, is the genus with the largest number of varieties. It is likely that many more will be discovered.

These orchids are at home on the slopes of the Himalayas, in southern China, lower India, Malaysia, Indonesia, the Philippines, New Guinea, Australia, and the Fiji Islands.

Dendrobium means "tree dweller," an indication that the plant is an epiphyte. This genus produces extremely rare colors and shapes. All of these orchids have pseudobulbs, and all are able to develop roots. *Dendrobium* do not grow single flowers, rather they have numerous cymes and loosely branched flower clusters. The flowers show an impressive palette of white, yellow, orange, red, pink, dark red, purple, violet, carmine, and, in some rare cases, even blue.

Some plants are evergreen; some are deciduous. Left on the plant, the flowers will last for two to three weeks.

Conditions for cultivation

The way *Dendrobium* orchids are watered must be adapted to the growing habits of the plant. If the relative humidity is too high, the plant will produce too much nectar, and the flower petals will stick together.

A good substrate consists of a mixture of fern root, bark, and a rigid plastic foam. Repotting should be done every three to four years. Orchids that flower in the spring should only be repotted after blooming is finished; for fall-flowering plants, this is done when shoots begin to appear. After repotting, the plant should be kept warm and be provided with additional humidity.

As far as temperatures are concerned, *Dendrobium* is divided into four groups:

1. Plants needing a cool climate

During the summer, the daytime temperatures should be 59 to 64°F (15 to 18°C) and at night, around 54°F (12°C). During the winter months, the daytime temperature should be 54°F (12°C), and the nighttime temperature 46°F (8°C).

This group of *Dendrobium* requires a daytime relative humidity of about 90 percent in the summer and a nighttime humidity of 60 to

80 percent. These orchids love light in the fall. The light intensity should be 50,000 lux in the summer and fall.

Dendrobium aggregatum
Pseudobulbs are 2¾ inches (7 cm) long, egg-shaped, and flattened; one leaf with floral axes of loosely branched clusters, trailing and developing from the uppermost bulb; flowers are 1¼ inches (3 cm) in diameter, golden yellow, and scented. Home: Burma and southern China, at elevations of 1,600 to 4,200 feet (500 to 1,200 m).

Dendrobium means "tree dweller."

85

Blooms from March to May.
Tip: Should be grown on a block.

Dendrobium chrysotoxum
Pseudobulbs are up to 10 inches (25 cm) long and spindle-shaped with a few leaves at the tips; flowers are usually upright, 8 inches (20 cm) long, carrying 6 to 12 golden yellow blossoms 1½ inches (4 cm) in diameter.
Home: Burma to southern China, at elevations of 2,300 to 3,300 feet (700 to 1,000 m).
Blooms from December to May.

Dendrobium parishii
Pseudobulbs are up to 10 inches (25 cm) long and cylindrical; floral axes develop on last year's pseudobulbs; flowers are 2 inches (5 cm) in diameter, pink to carmine red.
Home: Burma to southern China, at elevations of about 1,000 to 4,000 feet (300 to 1,200 m).
Blooms from May to June.
Tip: During active growth, keep plant warm and moist; during winter keep cool and less moist.

2. Plants needing a temperate climate

These orchids need a summer daytime temperature of 64 to 70°F (18 to 21°C) and nighttime temperatures of 54°F (12°C). During the winter months, the daytime temperatures should be 61 to 64°F (16 to 18°C), and nighttime temperatures should be 54°F (12°C).

The active growing period lasts from April to November or December. The plant is in bloom from February to May. Other conditions for cultivation are the same as for other plants that need a cool climate.

Dendrobium chrysanthum
Pseudobulbs are up to 3 feet (1 m) long; only a few golden yellow flowers will grow on previous year's pseudobulbs.
Home: Himalayas to Thailand, at elevations of 4,900 feet (1,500 m).
Blooms from March to September.
Tip: Dry, warm air presents a danger of red spider infection.

Dendrobium loddigesii
Pseudobulbs are thin, fleshy, and about 8 inches (20 cm) long; flowers are 1½ inches (4 cm) in diameter, light pink carmine; lip is golden yellow and white with carmine edging.
Home: Southern China.
Blooms from February to May.
Tip: Keep plant cool and moist in the winter.

Dendrobium primulinum
Pseudobulbs are up to 12 inches (30 cm) long and trailing; floral axes develop on older pseudobulbs and have one to two blossoms; flowers

Dendrobium loddigesii

are 1½ inches (4 cm) in diameter, color is light pink with carmine; lip is yellow with carmine edging.
Home: Nepal, Sikkim, and Burma; grows as an epiphyte at elevations of 1,000 to 4,000 feet (300 to 1,200 m). Blooms from February to May.
Tip: Keep plant warm and moist during the summer; cool and less moist during the winter.

Dendrobium loddigesii

Dendrobium superbum
Pseudobulbs are rod-shaped, trailing, and up to 28 inches (70 cm) long; one to two flowers grow from each shoot; flowers are up to 4 inches (10 cm) in diameter, pinkish carmine; lip is dark purple in the center.
Home: Malaysia, Borneo, and the Philippines.
Blooms from February to May.
Note: During the rest period in winter, the plant has no leaves.

3. Plants needing a warm climate
During the summer months, daytime temperatures should be around 64 to 82°F (18 to 29°C), while nighttime temperatures can be 61 to 70°F (16 to 21°C). Winter temperatures should be 68°F (20°C) during the day and 64°F (18°C) at night.

Dendrobium phalaenopsis
Pseudobulbs are up to 28 inches (70 cm) long with leaves on the upper portion; floral axes are upright and can be up to 6¼ inches (16 cm) long and have 12 blossoms; flowers can be up to 2¼ inches (6 cm) in diameter, carmine red; lip is dark purple; the species shows great variability.
Home: Northeastern Australia, in lower regions.

Dendrobium superbum

Dendrobium phalaenopsis

Blooms from September to January. Tip: During active growth, plant needs warmth around 72 to 77°F (22 to 25°C); in winter, during the day, around 64 to 68°F (18–20°C); nights should never be under 61°F (16°C).

4. Plants needing alternate warm and cool climate

Nighttime summer temperatures should be 54 to 64°F (12 to 18°C), and during the day, 59 to 75°F, (15 to 24°C). In winter, daytime tempera-

---

Dendrobium-Phalaenopsis Hybrids

Dendrobium-phalaenopsis hybrids are often cultivated in warehouses and offered to the public at affordable prices.

Den. Louis Bleriot (Den. phalaenopsis × Den. superbiens)

(Vacherot-Lecoufle, 1929)

Den. Lady Hamilton (Den. Diamond Head Beauty × Den. phalaenopsis)

Den. Pompadour (Den. Louis Bleriot × Den. Phalaenopsis)

Den. Maui-Beauty (Den. Lady Hamilton × Den. Helen Fukumura)

Den. American Beauty (Den. Anouk × Den. Lady Hamilton)

Dendrobium nobile

tures should be 54°F (12°C), and during the night about 41 to 46°F (5–8°C). During the time when the plant prepares for flowering, watering should be reduced, and from the beginning of November, temperatures should be lowered.

Dendrobium nobile
Lance-shaped leaves and strongly scented flowers that are 2 to 3¼ inches (5 to 8 cm) in diameter. Home: Southern China to Taiwan, Vietnam, and the Himalayan region. Blooms from January to April.

Dendrobium nobile and its hybrids
Pseudobulbs are up to 28 inches (70 cm) long, upright; floral axes have two to three blossoms; flowers are 2¼ inches (6 cm) in diameter, colors are carmine red and white at the base; lip is white with carmine

Dendrobium Nobile Hybrids
Den. Ainsworth (Den. heterocarpum × Den. nobile. 1864)
Den. Anne Marie (Den. Montrose × Den.
Winifried Fortesque Wichmann, 1963
Den. Cassiope (Den. moniliforme × Den. nobile, 1890)
Den. Glorious Rainbow (Den. Permos × Den. Valademos)
(Yamanoto, 1968)

89

red edges, mouth is light yellow with brown speckles.

Home: Himalayas to southern China and Taiwan, at elevations of 4,900 feet (1,500 m).

Blooms from February to May.

Tip: Keep plant cool in the winter; if the temperature during the winter can be kept at 50°F (10°C), the plant will produce flowers several times during the year.

Vanda and Its Relatives

Close relatives of *Vanda* are *Vandopsis*, *Arachnis*, *Ascocentrum*, and *Renanthera* (growing from Southeast Asia to Australia), as well as *Aërangis* and *Angraecum* (growing in Eastern Africa and Madagascar). They are epiphytes and lithophytes.

Vanda, the original Indian name for orchids, grows in regions ranging from India to the Philippines and consists of about 60 species. The plant is an epiphyte and produces abundant flowers. Flowers grow laterally, upright from the base of two-leaved shoots; leaves are usually strap-shaped but can also take other forms. Often several flowers are produced by one plant. This orchid is easy to cultivate. Crossbreeding of above-cited genera has produced many different species.

Conditions for cultivation

The genus *Vanda* prefers nighttime temperatures of about 61° to 64°F (16–18°C) and daytime temperatures of 64 to 75°F (18–24°C) during the summer months. The latter may also be higher. During the winter, temperatures cannot fall below 59°F (15°C). During active growth in the summer, *Vanda* orchids require a great deal of fresh air and good air circulation; relative humidity should be around 50 to 70 percent; however, the humidity should be high throughout the year so that the aerial roots are able to extract moisture from the air.

All *Vanda* orchids require much light (above 10,000 1ux) in order to produce flowers. A typical sign of too little light and too much water is strong leaf development at the expense of good flower development.

Vanda species

Vanda coerulea
Flowers are light blue with darker, chessboard markings, and grow on multi-flowered stalks.
Home: Himalayas to Burma, at elevations of about 2,600 to 5,900 feet (800 to 1,800 m).
Blooms from August to October.
Tip: Temperatures during the rest period should be 54°F (12°C).

Vanda sanderiana
(syn. *Euanthe sanderiana*)
Beautiful, large flowers on multi-blossom stalks; whitish pink and yellow brown colors and red veins.
Home: The Philippines.
Blooms throughout the year, but primarily in late summer.
Tip: Prefers a moist, warm climate.

Vanda tricolor
Scented, white yellow, three-lobed flowers with red brown speckles;

Vanda tricolor

Vanda Hybrids

These are important for orchid culti-vation in Southeast Asia. Flowers of countless species are imported as cut flowers.

Vanda Burgeffii (V. sanderiana × V. tri-color. 1928)

Vanda Miss Joaquim (V. hookerana × V. teres (first hybrid, 1893)

Vanda Rothschildiana (V. coerulea × V. sanderiana, 1931)

Recent hybrids: *Vanda Eisensander, Vanda Lenavat*

Vanda hybrid "Miss Joaquim"

red purple lip on multi-blossom stalks.
Home: Java to Australia.
Blooms from April to May or August to October, but produces flowers at other times.

Arachnis

This genus, closely related to *Renanthera*, is found in the Malaysian region. In Southeast Asia, these orchids and their hybrids are grown for cut flowers.

Conditions for cultivation

Daytime temperature (and humidity during the day and night) must be higher than for the *Vanda* orchid. This plant grows best in a heated greenhouse. The orchid needs to be watered at an even rate throughout the year.

Arachnis flos-aëris
Upright, two-leaved shoots; flower stalk can be 24 to 32 inches (60 to 80 cm) long; flowers are musk scented, color is yellow green, with purple brown stripes.
Home: Malaysia.

Important Arachnis Hybrid
Aranda Lucy Laycock (Arachnis hookeriana × Vanda tricolor)

Arachnis hookeriana

92

Blooms from September to November.

Arachnis hookeriana
Upright, two-leaved shoots; flower stalks are 24 to 32 inches (60–80 cm) long; scented flowers are cream white with purple speckles and stripes.
Home: Malaysia.
Blooms from August to October.

Ascocentrum

The five species of this genus come from Southeast Asia in regions ranging from Burma to Java, Celebes, and the Philippines. All plants are small. They are epiphytes and have dense leaf growth with mostly elongated leaves that are more or less fleshy and grow on upright stems. Flower stalks are upright, only moderately long, and produce many flowers with particularly striking colors.

Conditions for cultivation
Nighttime temperatures necessary for good growth are about 61 to 64°F (16 to 18°C). Daytime temperatures should be 70 to 84°F (21 to 29°C) with a relative humidity of at least 50 percent. A heated greenhouse is ideal, since light and temperature requirements can both be met, providing that a bright, sunny location is chosen. Excessive direct sunlight causes sunburn damage to leaves; therefore, it is important to provide sufficient shade during midday. Good air circulation is necessary. Like all other epiphytes, this orchid can be cultivated in baskets filled with fern root. However, it is also

Ascocentrum miniatum

possible to grow it in flowerpots in commercial orchid substrate.

Ascocentrum curvifolium
Color of the flower ranges from orange to scarlet.
Home: Himalayas, Assam, Burma, and Vietnam, at elevations of 1,000

Ascocentrum Hybrids

All *Ascocentrum* orchids have yellow orange or carmine red flowers; hybrids with *V. coerlea* are blue in color.
Ascocenda (Ascocentrum × Vanda, 1949)
Ascda. Meda Arnold (Asctm. curvifolium × Vanda Rothschildiana)
Ascocentrum (Asctm.) Sagarik Gold (Asctm. miniatum × Asctm. curvifolium, 1966)
Asconopsis Mini-Coral (Ascocentrum × Phalaenopsis schilleriana, 1968)
Yusoffara (Ascocentrum × Arachnis × Renanthera × Vanda, 1972)

93

to 3,300 feet (300 to 1,000 m).
Blooms from May to August.

Ascocentrum miniatum
Color of flowers is light orange to
vermilion red, rarely yellow.
Home: Himalayas and Sikkim to
Java, at elevations of 800 to 4,000 feet
(250 to 1,200 m).
Blooms from April to August.

Renanthera

This genus consists of 15 species and
is found in regions ranging from
eastern Asia and southern China to
the Solomon Islands.

Most species grow as epiphytes
in warm and sunny locations.
Shoots have two leaves, growing upright. The plant is densely covered
with leathery leaves that grow opposite each other, where it produces
long, upright floral axes with impressive flowers.

Conditions for cultivation

Renanthera prefers the environment
of a heated greenhouse. However,
R. imshootiana can tolerate cooler
temperatures.

In general, *Renanthera* grows well
with daytime temperatures of 70 to
84°F (21 to 29°C) and nighttime temperatures of 61 to 64°F (16 to 18°C).
The best temperatures for *R. imshootiana* are 64 to 82°F (18 to 28°C) during the day and 55°F (13°C) at night.

Relative humidity should be
around 70 percent; *R. imshootiana* can
tolerate lower humidity—about 50
percent. Proper air circulation must
be provided.

For good flowering, this genus
needs direct sunlight or strong artifi-

Renanthera imshootiana

cial light (at least 10,000 1ux), which is particularly important in the fall, at the end of the active growth period.

Plants need to be constantly moist during the active growth period; but they should never stand in water.

Renanthera can be propagated by dividing the upper portion of the stem of the plant; however, air roots should be present on that stem (see the information on vegetative propagation).

Renanthera coccinea
Climbing plant that can reach a height of 30 feet (9 m) in its native home; multiflowering; flowers can reach 2¼ inches (6 cm) in diameter, color is scarlet red, petals are light pink and red speckled; lip is yellow red with stripes.
Home: Burma to India.
Blooms from March to April.

Renanthera imshootiana
Shoots are 32 inches (80 cm) long, upright, and densely covered with leaves; petals are scarlet red; lip is yellow with salmon markings.
Home: Eastern India (particularly Assam) to Vietnam.
Blooms from July to August.

Renanthera Hybrids

Renades Kaiulani (Ren. monachica
  × *Aerides fieldineii*, 1955)
Has strikingly brilliant orange to red
  flowers.
Renantanda Titan (Ren. imshootiana
  × *Vanda sanderiana*, 1935)
Renanthopsis Premier (Ren. imshootiana
  × *Phal. sanderiana*, 1931)

Orchid Genera and Species for Orchid Lovers with Experience

Ada

Ada aurantiaca
This orchid is at home in regions ranging from Colombia to Venezuela. It is a relative of the *Odontoglossum.*
Blooms from January to May.

Conditions for cultivation
Ada aurantiaca is a member of the group of orchids that needs a cool environment. Nighttime temperatures around 43°F (6°C) are important. In addition, the plant needs much fresh air; otherwise, the care is the same as for *Odontoglossum.*

Aërangis

Aërangis (related to *Angraecum*), an epiphyte, is at home in the tropical regions of Africa and Madagascar. It consists of about 70 species. The single stem is stocky. The plant grows near water and blooms from late winter to spring.

Conditions for cultivation
Aërangis needs a warm to temperate environment and does not tolerate direct sunlight (if at all, only in winter). Otherwise, it needs the same care as *Angraecum* (see next page).

95

Ada aurantiaca

Aërangis friesiorum
The flowers are greenish white and scented.
Home: Kenya.
Blooms from April to July.

Aerides

Aerides odoratum
An epiphyte that grows near water at elevations of 500 to 1,000 feet (150 to 300 m), a relative of the genus *Vanda*; floral axes consist of cream white, fragrant flowers with pink violet speckles.
Home: Burma, Indochina, Malaysia, and the Philippines.
Blooms from May to August.

Conditions for cultivation
Daytime temperatures should be about 75°F (24°C), nighttime tem-

peratures about 64°F (18°C). This orchid requires a location that provides partial shade.

Angraecum

This genus is an epiphyte from tropical Africa and Madagascar. It has a monopodial stem that can reach 3 feet (1 m) in length with wide, arching leaves.

Conditions for cultivation
Angraecum is a perfect plant to grow on the windowsill or even in the cellar, since it requires partial shade. Ideal temperatures are 64 to 72°F (18 to 22°C) during the day and 55 to 61°F (13 to 16°C) at night. Relative humidity should be about 60 percent. The substrate must be evenly

Angraecum eburneum superbum

moist, and the plant should be fertilized with every third watering.

Angraecum eburneum superbum
Waxlike flowers are white to ivory colored.
Home: Rain forests of Madagascar. Blooms from December to April.

Ansellia

Ansellia africana
This genus belongs to the *Polystachia* family. It is monopodial and is found in the tropics of Africa, growing as an epiphyte at elevations of 300 to 2,600 feet (100 to 800 m). The flowers vary widely, and the colors are yellowish green with red speckles.

Conditions for cultivation
The daytime temperature during active growth should be 64 to 77°F (18 to 25°C) combined with a high relative humidity. Temperatures during the rest period should be no more than 59 to 64°F (15 to 18°C) with less humidity. This orchid will need a shaded location and sufficient amounts of fresh air. Reduce watering during the rest period, beginning in late summer. The substrate is the same as that normally used for epiphytes.

Aspasia

Aspasia lunata
This orchid, found in Brazil, grows as an epiphyte. It is similar to the genus *Odontoglossum*. The flower is greenish with brown speckles; the

97

Ansellia africana

Aspasia lunata

lip is white and violet in the center. Blooms from June to September.

Conditions for cultivation

During active growth, the plant needs temperatures from 64 to 68°F (18 to 20°C) with even humidity. During the rest period in winter, the temperature should be 61 to 64°F (16 to 18°C). Low temperatures are damaging. This orchid loves high relative humidity.

98

Barkeria spectabilis

Barkeria

Barkeria spectabilis
This epiphyte grows on oak trees in Central America at elevations of around 4,900 feet (1,500 m). It is a relative of the *Epidendrum* orchid; flowers are white to pink with darker speckles.
Blooms from April to August.

Conditions for cultivation
For best growth, daytime temperatures should be 59 to 68°F (15 to 20°C). During the rest period, temperatures of 50 to 59°F (10 to 15°C) are ideal. Nighttime temperatures should not go below 41°F (5°C). During the development of shoots, high temperatures support good growth. The only water the plant needs is supplied through spraying; the customary watering is not necessary. Little substrate is needed for cultivating this orchid.

Bifrenaria

The genus *Bifrenaria* consists of about 15 species found in the tropical forests of South America. They grow as epiphytes, as well as lithophytes, in large colonies. Pseudobulbs are square or egg-shaped and carry one leaf from which the beautiful flower develops.

Conditions for cultivation
During active growth, the plant

99

Bifrenaria harrisoniae

needs warm to temperate conditions. Nighttime temperature should be between 55 and 61°F (13 and 16°C); daytime temperatures must be between 64 and 75°F (18 and 24°C). During the winter, the temperatures should be 10°F (6°C) lower. Relative humidity must be at least 50 percent.

Bifrenaria harrisoniae
Flowers are waxlike with a strong fragrance; the color is ivory with a wine red lip.
Home: Brazil.
Blooms from March to June.

Brassia

This genus consists of about 50 species which range from Florida to the Antilles, Brazil, and Peru. They usually grow as epiphytes; in some instances, however, they are terrestrial. The shape of the plant, particularly that of the flowers, is very similar to *Odontoglossum* species.

Petals and sepals are long and thin. The lip, on the other hand, is mostly flat and much shorter. *Brassia* develop pseudobulbs that can be as long as 6 inches (15 cm).

Conditions for cultivation
Nighttime temperatures should be 55 to 61°F (13 to 16°C); daytime

100

Brassia verrucosa

should be 64 to 75°F (18 to 24°C). This genus is especially well suited for cultivation on a windowsill. The plants need a bright location, but they will not tolerate direct sunlight.

Relative humidity should be between 50 and 70 percent. During active growth, the plant needs sufficient water. The rest period should last about two months, during which watering is reduced. How-ever, the root bulb should not dry out completely. In addition, the plant needs to be kept cool during the rest period. In general, good air circulation is recommended. Fertilizer should be applied with every third watering, but only during the growth period.

Brassia verrucosa
Flowers are clustered, green with

101

Broughtonia sanguinea

dark brown speckles, and are tail shaped; the stems carry numerous white flowers; the lip is dark green. Home: Mexico to Venezuela; grows as an epiphyte at elevations of about 2,300 to 4,900 feet (700 to 1,500 m). Blooms from April to July.

Tip: It is essential for the plant to have a rest period before pseudo-bulbs are finished growing. This will initiate good flower development.

Brassia Hybrids

In the last three decades, *Brassia* hybrids have been crossbred with their relatives.

Here are a few examples:

Brassia × *Odontoglossum* = *Odontobrassia*

Brassia × *Oncidium* = *Brassidium*

Brassia × *Cochlioda* × *Miltonia* × *Odontoglossum* = *Beallara*

Broughtonia

Broughtonia sanguinea

A favorite species for crossbreeding with *Cattleya*, because of the brilliant purple, carmine, and red colors of its flowers. Conditions for cultivation are similar to those of the *Cattleya*. Sufficient fertilization is essential for good growth and flower development.

Home: Jamaica and Cuba; grows as an epiphyte and as a lithophyte.

Blooms from October to February.

Calanthe

The genus *Calanthe* ranges from South Africa, Madagascar, and the tropics of Asia to Australia and Tahiti. There are about 150 species. Sepals and petals are almost identical in shape and size. The large, angular pseudobulbs with their narrow middle are unique features of this genus. Most *Calanthe* orchids are terrestrial plants.

Conditions for cultivation

These orchids prefer daytime temperatures of 64 to 70°F (18 to 21°C) and nighttime temperatures around 57°F (14°C). A relative humidity of 40 to 60 percent is ideal. A shaded location and good air circulation are necessary. During the rest period, after flowering has stopped, the plant must be kept completely dry. Discontinue feeding at this time. When blooming stops (at the end of the year), the deciduous *Calanthe* can be kept in a dark and dry location (under a bench) until new shoots begin to appear (beginning of March). At the beginning of the growth period, the plant must be watered regularly and fertilized with every second watering. Leaves should not become

102

Calanthe vestita

wet. As soon as the leaves start to yellow, discontinue watering.

Calanthe vestita
Color and size of the orchid vary widely.
Home: Burma to southern Vietnam and Borneo to Celebes.
Blooms from October to February.

Calanthe Hybrids

Cal. masuca × *Cal. furcata* = *Cal. Dominyi*, 1854
This was the first artificially produced orchid hybrid.
C. Sedeni (Cal. veitchii × *Cal. vestita)*

Coelogyne

Coelogyne massangeana
This orchid has long, trailing floral axes; flowers are whitish to light ochre yellow with brown speckles.

Coelogyne massangeana

103

Home: Assam, Sumatra, and Java. Blooms from March to June.

Conditions for cultivation

A temperate to cool climate is required. Relative humidity should be 40 to 70 percent. To encourage development of flowers, the rest period must be strictly observed. During this time, the plant must be kept cool and dark and receive only a very limited amount of water.

Cymbidium

This genus consists of 40 species and is found in the Himalayas, Indochina, China, Japan, New Guinea, and Australia. The orchids grow as epiphytes or as terrestrial plants. Almost all species develop egg-shaped to elongated pseudobulbs. In some, the development of bulbs is very limited and is surrounded by dense leaf growth. Thick, fleshy roots are covered by velamen, a corky outer tissue that quickly absorbs water from the air. Flowers grow upright, horizontally, or trailing from below the axis of the pseudobulbs. Most

Cymbidium lowianum.

species go into bloom in February. If the plant is kept in a cool place, it will bloom for 12 weeks. The long, small leaves will last for several years.

Conditions for cultivation

Most *Cymbidium* species need a temperate climate during active growth. During the rest period, however, cool temperatures are better. Nighttime temperatures during the summer should be about 50 to 55°F (10 to 13°C); daytime temperatures should be 61 to 75°F (16 to 24°C).

Flowering is initiated by lowering nighttime temperatures. The temperature difference between day and night should be at least 18°F (10°C). As soon as flower buds begin to appear, nighttime temperature should not exceed 57°F (14°C), otherwise the plant will lose the buds. Only miniature *Cymbidium* can tolerate higher temperatures, as can *Cattleya* orchids.

Relative humidity should be at least 50 to 60 percent. Direct sunlight won't harm the plant if it is shaded during midday. The orchid will tolerate outside locations well in a mild climate.

Cymbidium orchids thrive in an oversized pot that provides room for the fast-growing roots.

A substrate mixture of bark, coarse peat moss, or Osmunda fibre, and sand or gravel works well, but commercial orchid substrates can also be used.

During active growth, *Cymbidium* needs to be watered well; however, overwatering should be avoided. Infrequent watering during the rest period helps to avoid dehydration of leaves and pseudobulbs.

Cymbidium lowianum
Bears about 10 flowers on panicles (pyramidal, loosely branched flower clusters). Flowers are about 4 inches (10 cm) wide. Sturdy green yellow, yellow reddish lipped blossoms.
Home: Burma.
Blooms from February through April.

Cymbidium traceyanum
The 6-inch-wide olive green blossoms are borne on a multiflowered panicle. The blossoms have a light yellow, purple brownish flecked edge.
Home: Burma.
Blooms from October through December.

Mini Cymbidium Hybrids
Angelika "Advent"
Avers Rock "Cooksbridge Velvet"
Baltic
Fort George "Lewes"
Gymer "Cooksbridge"
Pearl Balkis "Fiona"

Miniature Cymbidium hybrid

105

Gongora

Gongora galeata
An epiphyte with a multiflowering, trailing stem and yellow brown flowers.
Home: Mexico.
Blooms from July to August.

Conditions for cultivation

During active growth, temperatures should be 64 to 75°F (18 to 24°C) during the day and 54 to 64°F (12 to 18°C) at night. During the rest period in winter, the temperature should be about 61°F (16°C). The root bulbs should be kept moderately moist. This epiphyte requires a porous, humus substrate. Flower stems are able to develop well when allowed to trail.

Leptotes

The home of this genus, which is composed of only a few species, ranges from Brazil to Paraguay.

Leptotes is very similar in its habits to *Brassavola*. It is a small epiphyte, and the small pseudobulbs have only one leaf each. In contrast, the flowers are relatively large and grow on short stems. This orchid does well on a windowsill.

Conditions for cultivation

These orchids need temperate conditions. Temperatures should be 64

Gongora galeata

to 75°F (18 to 24°C) during the day and 55 to 61°F (13 to 16°C) at night. A relative humidity of 40 to 60 percent is ideal. Plants need shade and good air circulation.

Leptotes can be cultivated as an epiphyte on a tree branch or terrestrially in a flowerpot. A substrate mixture of bark, Osmunda fibre, and peat moss is recommended. The potting mix should be allowed to dry out between waterings. Fertilizer should be applied at every third watering.

Leptotes bicolor
A single white flower on each stem with a violet pink lip.
Home: Brazil and Paraguay, in rain

forests at elevations of 3,300 feet (1,000 m).
Blooms from January to April.

Leptotes unicolor
Floral axis with two to three violet pink flowers.
Home: Brazil.
Blooms in February, after the rest period.

Lycaste

The genus *Lycaste* consists of 40 species and is found from Mexico and the Antilles to Peru and Brazil. It grows primarily as an epiphyte at

Leptotes bicolor

higher elevations in regions with high humidity.

Conditions for cultivation

Temperatures at night of 50 to 55°F (10 to 13°C) and during the day of 61 to 64°F (16 to 18°C) are best for this orchid. Relative humidity should be 40 to 60 percent.

The genus *Lycaste* loves light in shaded locations that provide sufficient air circulation. Fertilizer should be applied with every third watering. During the rest period, do not fertilize, and water only sparingly. As substrate, use a mixture of bark, peat moss, Osmunda fibre, and a rigid plastic foam. The best time for repotting is after the plant has finished blooming, but only if the substrate has deteriorated.

Lycaste aromatica
Single scented flower, greenish orange, yellow in color.
Home: Central America to Honduras, at elevations of 2,600 to 5,900 feet (800 to 1,800 m).
Blooms from March to May.

Lycaste virginalis (L. skinneri)
This orchid has been totally protected in its homeland; has white to pink red flowers.
Home: Mexico at elevations of 4,900 to 6,600 feet (1,500 to 2,000 m).
Blooms from October to March.

Lycaste Hybrids
Lycaste × *Anguola* = *Angulocaste*
Lycaste × *Zygopetalum* = *Zygocaste*
Angulocaste Sanderae = *Ang. clowesii*
  × *Lyc. skinneri*
Blooms in the winter and spring.

Lycaste aromatica

108

Maxillaria

The home of this genus reaches all the way from Florida and Mexico to Central America and Argentina. Most of the 300 species grow as epiphytes, but some are lithophytes, and some grow terrestrially. Many different forms are represented in this large group, such as small species with creeping rhizomes and others with large, long floral axes.

The fragrance, large size, and color of the flowers are often very striking, but they can also be very unattractive. The flower stem develops at the rhizome near a new shoot and generally carries only one flower.

Conditions for cultivation

Most of the cultivated species need nighttime temperatures of 55 to 61°F (13 to 16°C) and daytime temperatures of 64 to 75°F (18 to 24°C). A relative humidity of 40 to 60 percent and good air circulation are necessary for good growth.

A location with bright but diffused lighting (corresponding to the conditions in the plant's original home) is best for this orchid. Either tree branches or a flowerpot can be used for the plant. As substrate, use a mixture of bark, Osmunda fibre, coarse peat moss, and a rigid plastic foam. The substrate must be evenly moist during the active growth period. All species are fertilized with every third watering.

Reduce watering during the rest period to avoid harming the plant. However, the substrate should not dry out completely. Do not fertilize during this time. Repot at the very beginning of the active growth period.

Maxillaria picta

Maxillaria luteo-alba
Flower is whitish and yellow brown; lip has red markings.
Home: Central America.
Blooms from April to July.

Maxillaria picta
Flower is whitish and yellow brown; lip is horizontally striped in purple brown and has white and red speckles.
Home: Brazil.
Blooms from January till April.

Vanilla

Vanilla planifolia
This orchid is known for its vanilla pods. It is an ideal plant for the connoisseur. In order to produce pods, the larger, yellow green flowers have to be artificially pollinated. Pods need 10 months to ripen.
Home: Central and South America.
Blooms from July to August.

Vanilla planifolia

Conditions for cultivation

Temperatures during the summer should be 64 to 75°F (18 to 24°C); during the winter they should be about 59 to 64°F (15 to 18°C). High humidity is recommended. This orchid can be grown on the branch of an oak tree.

Zygopetalum

The approximately 20 species of the genus *Zygopetalum* are found in Trinidad, at the northern part of South America to Peru, and from northern Argentina to Peru. They grow as epiphytes and lithophytes.

Small leaves grow at the tip of each elliptical pseudobulb. The upright stems usually carry very pleasantly scented flowers that look like stars—the sepals and petals have similar shapes. The large, fan-shaped middle lobe of the lip is characteristic of *Zygopetalum*.

Conditions for cultivation

The *Zygopetalum* orchid prefers temperatures that range at night from 55 to 61°F (13 to 16°C) and from 64 to 75°F (18 to 24°C) during the day. Direct sunlight should be avoided if possible; diffuse light corresponds best to the location of this plant's original home. Relative humidity should be 40 to 60 percent.

Commercial substrate mixtures used for epiphytes can be used for the *Zygopetalum* species. However, a mixture of coarse peat moss, sandy loam, bark, and a rigid plastic foam is also very good.

During active growth, the substrate should be kept evenly moist. During the rest period, it should only

Zygopetalum mackayi

Orchids That Need Little Energy

The following is a list of very adaptable orchids. They are satisfied with minimum nighttime temperatures of 50°F (10°C) and can tolerate maximum daytime temperatures of 95°F (35°C): Miniature *Cymbidium* species from eastern Asia, as well as *Cymbidium* hybrids *Dendrobium fimbriatum, D. kingianum, D. linguiforme, D. loddigesii, D. nobile, D. thyrsiflorum,* and *D. speciosum; Encyclia*

be watered if it has completely dried out. Because of its dense leaf covering, the *Zygopetalum* plant is particularly susceptible to rot.

Zygopetalum crinitum
Produces five to seven green brown speckled flowers on one stem; lip has brown violet stripes.
Home: Brazil.
Blooms from November to February.

Zygopetalum mackayi
Flowers are similar to *Zygopetalum crinitum.*
Home: Brazil.
Blooms from November to February.

Zygopetalum maxillare
Grows exclusively as an epiphyte; flowers are green with brown speckles; lip is light blue to violet.
Home: Brazil and Paraguay.
Blooms from May to June.

Zygopetalum Hybrid
Zyg. Artur Elle = Zyg. blackii
  × *Zyg. B. G. White*
Blooms from September to January.

Laelia anceps is an orchid that tolerates somewhat low temperatures.

111

citrina, E. cochleata, E. mariae, E. nem-oralis; Epidendrum anceps; Laelia al-bida, L. anceps; L. autumnalis, L. su-perbiens; Schomburgkia superbiens; Lycaste aromatica, L. deppei; Miltonia spectabilis; Rossioglossum grande, R. insleayi; Odontoglossum rossii, O. uro-skinneri; Oncidium caven-dishianum, O. flexuosum, O. leuco-chilum, O. ornitthorhynchum, O. ti-grinum; Paphiopedilum fairieanum, P. insigne, P. villosum; Vanda cristata; Zygopetalum mackayi.

Hybrids

Vuylstekeara Cambria "Plush"
Vuylstekeara Edna (Miltonidia Har-woockii × Odontioda Charlesworthii)
Vuylstekeara Jaquelin
  (Vuyl. Cambria × Odontioda Lydia)

Plants That Go Well with Orchids

Plants that are interesting from a visual point of view and that go well with orchids are:
Acalypha such as *Acalypha hispida* and *A. wilkesiana*
Anthurium, Aglaoema, Dieffenbachia, and *Rhaphidophora*
Asparagus such as *Asparagus setaceus*
Begonia such as *Begonia Rex, B. cor-allina,* and *B. metallica*
Croton-Codiaeum
Dracaena such as *Dracaena marginata*
Epipremnum (syn. *Scindapsus*) and *Philodendron*
Ferns such as *Blechnum, Platycerium,*

Lygodium, Polypodium, and many others
Ficus
Fittonia
Gesnerien such as *Episcia cupreata* and others
Hippoestes
Indoor palms
Maranta
Pelargonium such as *Pelargonium graveolens* and *P. odoratissimum*
Schefflera
Selaginella such as *Selaginella apoda* and *S. martensii*

Climbing Plants

These plants are beautiful "frames" for orchids. The following should be considered:
Cissus such as *Cissus antarctica, C. danica,* and others
Clerodendrum
Hoya
Passiflora
Stephanotis floribunda
Tetrastigma vionieranaum

Other Epiphytes: Bromelia

The *Bromelia* plant comes from Central and South America. It takes in water and nutrients via its leaves. It does this with the help of suctorial scales located on the surface of the leaves. The funnel-like indentation of these scales should always be filled with water. This is why this plant is also called "cistern plant."

When *Bromelia* plants are grown in a flowerpot, it is important to use a substrate that drains well. Each plant blooms only once. Propagate by using rhizomes or seeds. Propagation through seeding is very diffi-

112

cult, so the vegetative method is recommended. The offspring should remain on the mother plant until roots have developed. They can then be cut off with a sharp knife. The offspring are allowed to dry out for several days until the cutting surface

begins to swell, an indication that new roots are developing.

If epiphytes are to be propagated via seeds, it is best to use branches from oak trees, since they last the

Orchids with companion plants

113

longest. Branches from the calabash tree (*Crescentia cujete*) are also very good. The gardener can grow these and use them as the base for epiphytes.

These *Bromelia*, which need temperate to warm conditions, are recommended:

Aechmea fasciata, A. maculata
Ananas comosus "Tricolor"
Billbergia mirabilis, B. nutans, B. vittata
Canistrum amazonicum (syn.
Wittrockia amazonica), *C. lindenii*
Cryptanthus undulatus, C. zonatus
Hohenbergia stellata
Guzmania lingulata, G. minor

Orchids, Bromelia, and other companion plants

114

Orchids as Cut Flowers

As flowers, orchids have become more and more popular over the years. Today, no flower shop would be without them. Surely, their exotic beauty, the fact that they last so long, and their brilliant colors are not the only reasons for this popularity.

However, not all orchids are equally suited for cut flowers. Some wilt within hours after cutting; others will last one or two months.

Some orchids, particularly *Paphiopedilum*, *Cymbidium*, and *Phalaenopsis*, are used in corsages because they last so long. *Cattleya* orchids are also used for such arrangements; however, their flowers don't last quite as long. Using air transport, cut orchids are imported directly from Southeast Asia, Australia, South Africa, and Central and South America. These imports include the very precious *Vanda* orchid. *Dendrobium phalaenopsis* and all

A wedding corsage

its hybrids are also available. It is a relatively robust and affordable orchid.

Certain characteristics can be used to determine if a cut orchid will last long. If the flower petals are rigid or even hard, if they have a sheen, or if they are coated with wax, it is safe to assume that they will last. If, however, the petals are soft, and the surface is dull, they will not last very long. If the petals have a glassy look, or if the veins of the leaves begin to protrude, they will wilt in a short time.

Some tips on care: Cut the stem of the flower at an angle under running water and use boiled water or water that has had time to settle. In any case, the flower must be protected against draft and too much heat. The water in the vase need not be changed; it is sufficient to add water as it evaporates. In order to let the plant absorb water, it is best to make a new cut at the end of the stem every two to three days.

Appendix

Flowering Calendar of the Orchids Discussed in This Book

Aspasia lunata

A

Ada aurantiaca	January to May
Aërangis friesiorum	April to June
Aërides odoratum	May to August
Angraecum eburneum	December to April
Ansellia africana	March to November
Arachnis flos-aëris	September to November
A. hookeriana	August to October

Ascocentrum curvifolium	May to August
A. miniatum	April to August
Aspasia lunata	June to September

B

Barkeria spectabilis	April to August
Bifrenaria harrisoniae	March to June

Stewartara Golden Star (Ada aurantiaca × Oda. Mainaustern)

Comparettia speciosa

Dendrobium loddigesii

B. verrucosa	April to June
Brassavola cucullata	Summer and fall
B. nodosa	Summer and winter
Broughtonia sanguinea	October to February

C

Calanthe vestita	October to February
Cattleya aclandiae	June to September
C. aurantiaca	April to June
C. dowiana	August to October
C. loddigesii	July to October
C. schilleriana	July to October
C. skinneri	March to November
Cochlioda neozliana	December to April
Coelogyne massangeana	March to June
Comparettia falcata	June to September
Cymbidium lowianum	February to April
C. tracayanum	October to December

D

Dendrobium aggregatum	March to May
D. chrysanthum	March to September
D. chrysotoxum	December to May
D. loddigesii	February to May
D. nobile	January to April
D. parishii	May to June
D. phalaenopsis	September to January
D. primulinum	February to May
D. superbum	February to May

E

E. mariae	Summer
E. vitellina	Summer and fall
Epidendrum (= Auliza) ciliare	Winter or late summer
E. radicans	All year, mostly in winter

G

Gongora galeatea	June to September

L

L. harpophylla	Winter and spring

L. purpurata	Spring		
Leptotes bicolor	January to April		
L. unicolor	February		
Lycaste aromatica	March to May		
L. virginalis	October to March		

M

Maxillaria luteo-alba	April to June
M. picta	January to April
Miltonia candida	August to October
M. spectabilis	July to October

Paphiopedilum niveum

O

Odontoglossum bictoniense	October to April	*P. argus*	March to June
O. cordatum	July to August	*P. bellatulum*	April to August
O. crispum	February to June	*P. callosum*	March to July
O. rossii	January to May	*P. delenatii*	March to June
Oncidium crispum	August to December	*P. fairieanum*	October to December
O. pulchellum	June to August	*P. hennisianum*	February to June
O. splendidum	December to February	*P. hirsutissimum*	February to June
		P. hookerae	April to June
O. triquetrum	August to October	*P. insigne*	November to January
O. varicosum	September to February	*P. mastersianum*	April to July
		P. niveum	July to November
		P. parishii	April to September
P		*P. philippinense*	June to August
Paphiopedilum acmodontum	March to June	*P. praestans*	June to August
		P. sukhakulii	March to July

Odontocidium (Odm. uro-skinneri × Onc. anderanum)

P. tonsum	February to July	P. mariae	June to September
P. urbanianum	February to July		
P. villosum	November to February	P. sanderiana	December to July
Phalaenopsis amabilis	October to July (all year)	P. schilleriana	November to March
P. cornu-cervi	April to October (all year)	P. stuartiana	November to March
P. equestris	May to October (all year)	P. sumatrana	August to November
P. lueddemanniana	April to October	P. violacea	June to November
P. mannii	March to July		

Phalaenopsis

120

R

Renanthera coccinea	March to April
R. imshootiana	June to August
Rhyncholaelia digbyana	Spring to fall
R. glauca	Late winter to spring
Rossioglossum (Odontoglossum) grande	September to December

S

Sch. tibinicus	Spring and summer
Sophronitis coccinea	Winter and spring

V

Vanda coerulea	August to October
V. sanderiana	January to December, mainly in late summer
V. tricolor	April to May or August to October
Vanilla planifolia	July to August

Z

Zygopetalum crinitum	November to February
Z. mackayi	November to February
Z. maxillare	May to June

Wilsonara (Cochlioda hybrid)

Zygopetalum mackayi

Glossary

A
Aerial roots: Roots produced above or out of the substrate or potting mix.

B
Bifoliate: A plant with two leaves for each bulb.
Bud: The first step of flower development, initiated by outside forces, for instance, light and temperature.

C
Column: The organ in which the anther and stigma are fused together.

D
Deciduous: A plant that sheds its leaves at the end of the growth period.

E
Epiphyte: A plant growing on another plant or object, i.e., on trees.

G:
Genera: The plural of genus. A subdivision of a family having one or more related species.
Grex: All the offspring of a hybridized plant.

H
Hybrid: A plant produced by crossbreeding.

Dendrobium phalaenopsis hybrids as cut flowers men

Phalaenopsis orchids on shelves

I

Intergeneric hybrid: A product of crossbreeding two different genera.

K

Keiki: A Hawaiian term for the offshoot produced on the stem, spike, or base of an orchid.

L

Labellum: Lip, a specially developed petal.

Lithophyte: A plant that grows on rocks.

M

Monopodial: A plant with a main axis from which offshoots are formed.

Mycorrhiza fungus: A fungus that is essential for the germination of orchid seeds.

P

Petals: The inner leaves of a flower.

Pistil: The female organ of the plant, which produces the seeds.

Primary hybrid: The product of crossbreeding between two species of the same genus.

Pseudobulbs: The thickened aerial stem or shoot.

R

Rhizome: The subterranean stem or shoot.

S

Sepals: The outer leaves of a flower.

Stamen: The male organ of the plant, which produces pollen.

Substrate: The potting mix or mixture.

Sympodial: A plant with a common axis; new shoots develop from the base of previous growth.

T

Terrestrials: Plants that grow in the soil.

U

Unifoliate: A plant which has only one leaf per pseudobulb; for instance, *Cattleya* orchids.

V

Velamen: The thick, corky, moisture-absorbing covering of aerial roots.

Index